CULT OF APHRODITE

RITES AND FESTIVALS OF THE GOLDEN ONE

LAURELEI BLACK

© 2010, Asteria Books
Martinville, IN

CULT OF APHRODITE

RITES AND FESTIVALS OF THE GOLDEN ONE

LAURELEI BLACK

Project Editor: Laurelei Black
Cover Design: Natalie Long
Illustrator: Natalie Long

Black, Laurelei
Cult of Aphrodite: Rites and Festivals of the Golden One.
ISBN 1451527268
EAN-13 9781451527261

Keywords
1. Aphrodite 2. Hellenismos 3. Hellenic polytheism

Copyright © 2010 by Asteria Books

The individual works contained within this book are the sole intellectual property of the artists and writers whose names are credited herein. You may not reproduce, store or transmit any part of this book without the express written consent of the author or artist whose work you wish to use.

CONTENTS

Preface	7
A Guide to Greek Ritual	11
Decking the Temple, Shrine and Altar	23
Prayer	33
The Festival Calendar	35
Daily Lustration	42
Weekly Meditation	44
Monthly Offering	47
Feast of Eros	51
Rite of Peace	57
Anagogia	63
Katagogia	69
Arrephoria	75
Aphrodisia	83
Vinalia Rustica	91
Adonia	95
Epitymbria	101
Symposium of the Hetaerae	109
Bibliography	115
Appendix: Hymns to Aphrodite	119

Φεστιβάλ και αποχωρήσεις από τη Χρυσή
FESTIVALS AND RITES FOR THE GOLDEN ONE

πρόλογος
PREFACE

When I began my work with Aphrodite, I scoured the Internet and bookstore shelves looking for usable rituals, meditations, festival information – anything that would serve as a practical guide for worshipping and honoring Her. Sadly, I found very little.

Of the few authors who discuss Her, most write the Golden Kypriot off as some sort of fluff-ball Hellenic cheerleader/prom queen type of snob who holds such a low station in Greek theology that She didn't merit major civic festivals. The truth is that She was honored and revered in every wedding ceremony, in every bed, in the mourning of a lost love, in childbirth, and in more ways than we currently imagine. Her sphere of influence is far-reaching and significant, but Her's was viewed as a *private*, not civic, realm in most regions. Very few private pious practices remain for us, though, so we are required to recreate a both public and private practices for ourselves, if we wish to honor Her.

Contemporary writers seem to have overlooked and ignored Aphrodite's scope and significance, and they have left a gap in the body of Hellenic Polytheist and Neo-Pagan liturgy – a gap that needs to be filled with Her presence.

Aphrodite did have a few historically documented festivals that we can draw on, and She was traditionally included as a minor focus in the festivals of other Deities. Taking these

7

few resources and combining them with what we can extrapolate of Aphrodite from personal observations, we can create and cull a workable schedule of daily, weekly, and monthly rites and a round of festivals that covers the entire calendar year.

I've attempted to create liturgy with the help of the Cult of Aphrodite Asteria, Starry Queen of Heaven. This liturgical body provides a working model for groups and individuals to honor Her without having to sift through the complete corpus of Greek liturgy and research in order to find the relevant gems.

In truth, there may be more rituals in honor of a single Deity included in this volume than some folks need. However, my intention is to provide as complete a resource for the Aphrodisian worshipper in search of materials as I can compile. These rituals come from many parts of Hellas and some are modern innovations. A few express Graeco-Roman syncretism at their roots, as well.

I should give the disclaimer that I am not as strict a Hellenic Reconstructionist as some of my friends and peers, but I have attempted to present a ritual style that reflects a Hellenic sensibility, even where it may innovate. These are rituals that I have done, and these are the festivals that the Cult of Aphrodite Asteria has developed for its own use. As with any ritual that you find in a book, please "use, lose or abuse" any of the particular points of content and aesthetics that will help the rites work for you. After all, nothing that I've written is infallible Holy Writ. Aphrodite will be happier with the wording, styling and slant that help *you* to reach Her. Frankly, it is my belief that She, like all the Gods of Olympos, are happy to have us turn our devotion to them, even if we mortals can't always agree on the right ways to express said devotion.

Furthermore, I want to be clear about the fact that these rituals are my best attempts at constructing relevant liturgy for today from what little is known from the past. No complete outlines or scripts exist from Hellenic rites to show us exactly how these rituals happened. We have the "idea" of the festival or the rite, perhaps some historical blurb in a text or two, sculpture and pottery depictions of a few rites, and that is all the Cult of Aphrodite Asteria had to build from. I am not proposing that any of these rituals are genuine recreations of any ceremonies from the past. Some are entirely modern constructs, in fact. However, I try to provide the relevant historical, cultural and social information in the "Background" section of each ritual so that you understand what prompted the rite's inclusion in the book.

Ritual speaks to our psyches by communicating through symbol, poetry, movement, music, shared experience and emotion. Rituals, by definition, are acts that we repeat in order to achieve a given goal, and in the case of religious ritual, we are hoping to come to some sort of understanding or enlightenment regarding (and through) our shared experience. We are also giving something to the Gods via ritual — offerings (physical gifts) and devotion. I've attempted to layer symbol, poetry, movement and the rest as richly and deeply as possible to reach these goals. As such, these rituals offer distinctly different types of experience than providing a more direct, prosaic meditation or discussion would have done.

Φεστιβάλ και αποχωρήσεις από τη Χρυσή
FESTIVALS AND RITES FOR THE GOLDEN ONE

Οδηγός για την ελληνική Ιεροτελεστία
A GUIDE TO GREEK RITUAL

For those interested in recreating entirely authentic Greek rituals, there are several books on the market that lay out ritual philosophies and practices in very clear detail. Walter Burkert's *Greek Religion* is one text that comes to mind as an invaluable resource for understanding the form and function of ancient ritual practices. *Gods of the Greeks* by Karl Kerenyi will provide you with the mythological background needed, if you are lacking the stories needed to engage fully in the rituals. *A Beginner's Guide to Hellenismos* by Timothy Jay Alexander is another useful text, offering a practical interpretation since it speaks directly to the modern Hellenic Polytheist. *Kharis: Hellenic Polytheism Explored* by Sarah Kate Istra Winter is also an excellent resource for contemporary practice, giving the reader a slightly different view of the religion as it is practiced today.

The rituals presented in this liturgical compilation may not be viewed as entirely historically accurate. Because I came from a Neo-Pagan background, and I know that a great many of the current Aphrodisians aren't practicing Hellenic religion, I've focused my efforts on including those practices that speak most readily to a general practitioner's psyche with the smallest need for full, historical research and immersion. My goal is to have provided opportunities for deep philosophical reflection and study beyond the rites themselves, while still providing an experience that is full and complete in itself. In other words, these rituals should be approachable and digestible to most people, whether they are practicing Hellenes, Neo-Pagans, or Wiccans.

CULT OF APHRODITE

A quick discussion of practices for those who may be unfamiliar with Greek ritual, then, should suffice.

LIBATION

Offering food and drink to the Deities and ancestors is actually a common occurrence within almost all Pagan circles. Its need is obvious and its application is abundant. The "cakes and ale" ceremony that ends most Pagan/Wiccan rites is an example of a well-known libation.

The Greeks, however, delineated a couple of different needs and practices for libation. Nearly all of our rituals will incorporate what is known as *sponde* – a controlled pour to the ground. In *sponde*, not all of the liquid needs to be poured. *Sponde* is a shared drink in which the pourer also takes a drink of the liquid and, in this way, shares with the Gods. Conversely, there are a few instances in which the complete and passionate *khoe* is appropriate. *Khoe* involves spilling or dumping the liquid offering so that none remains inside the container. These offerings usually involve larger jugs of wine or water and are offered to the ancestors and underworld Gods.

You may not want to pour either type of libation onto the floor of your home, and you might even have thoughtful objections to libating alcohol to the ground outside. There are actually a couple of options for modifying at least the *sponde*. The use of a libation bowl into which you pour the liquid is one such alteration. An "internal" libation is another. For an internal libation, you drink the wine yourself.

FESTIVALS AND RITES FOR THE GOLDEN ONE

To some, this will sound like cheating. For others, it will make perfect sense.

PROCESSION

One of the key features of Greek festivals is the procession of the participants to the ritual site. This parade of ritual leaders, musicians, and townspeople marks the beginning of the festival, and it sets the tone for the rite to follow.

Called a *pompe*, the procession may be one of revelry or one of sobriety. It is probably not going to be silent, though, as music and dance have always been key elements for establishing the atmosphere.

The following rituals all suggest drumming, chanting and singing as ways to musically accompany the *pompe*. Use whatever tools are available to you for this. Panpipes, recorders, finger cymbals, ankle bells – a good deal of recorded music works well, both traditional and contemporary.

The physical pacing of the *pompe* does a lot to influence the ritual as well. A slower step establishes the somber quality of a funerary rite. A bouncy, dancing step or a slightly quick pace can accentuate the joy and playfulness of a joyous celebration.

Most of the ancient processional dances of the Greeks seem to have been line dances that greatly resemble the "grapevine."

Λατρεία της Αφροδίτης
CULT OF APHRODITE

FEAST

Feasting is an essential part of Greek ritual. The word "festival" actually derives from "feast," and all of the civic rituals of the Greeks included the sacrifice of an animal whose entrails would've been read for omens, fat and inedible parts burned as an offering to the Gods, and meat roasted for the community feast.

Now, we have a little debate about the propriety of live sacrifice on Aphrodite's altars. Empedocles tells us that Aphrodite is repulsed by bloodshed in Her rites. Of course, live sacrifice isn't a common practice in Neo-Hellenic rites, so that issue may not truly pose any moral dilemmas. However, we do have to consider whether it is appropriate to include meat in the feasts for the Kypriot.

My personal view is that vegetarianism wasn't a common practice among the ancient Hellenes. Though it was practiced by some people, such as the Orphics, it was still not the norm. So it is likely that an animal still would have been slaughtered for the communal feast. For this reason, I can't imagine that carnivorous dishes at a contemporary feast would be inappropriate for Aphrodisian celebration.

The one exception to this statement can be made in regards to pork. We are told that Aphrodite finds pork to be offensive and unclean, so we shouldn't offer it up at Her feasts.

SANCTITY OF THE TEMENOS

The *temenos* is the sacred space – the temple or the grove –

in which members of the cult or community would come together to celebrate and honor the rites of the Gods. Each *temenos* was sacred to a specific Deity, and each was maintained by the priesthood or community.

Your *temenos* is likely to be a site that is used for other activities as well. Your living room may function as the house of the Goddess for an evening, but in the morning it will go back to being the place where you watch television, talk to your friends, and read books.

If you are lucky enough to have a dedicated space, you can take the Greek attitude about its inherent sanctity. It will not require a fresh cleansing before every ritual. Perhaps you will cleanse it once per year, but you won't need to do it every time you approach the place.

If, like most of us, you must convert your living room, bedroom or backyard for ritual use, you may want to do something to clear it of profane energies. This simply means sending away the common, everyday energies in order to make way for the sacred.

The method used for this is simple. Sprinkle lustral water (*khernips*) over the altar and the area to be used in ritual. Lustral water is simply pure water — water from a natural, flowing source like a spring. You can use bottled spring water. You can also purify tap water with sea salt and a flaming branch (lit incense stick).

Λατρεία της Αφροδίτης
CULT OF APHRODITE

PERSONAL CLEANSING

Personal cleanliness was of utmost importance to each and every participant of ancient Greek rites. No person would consider entering the temple without having bathed and dressed in clean clothing. Furthermore, a ritual participant known as the *hydrophoros*, or water-bearer, would have poured water over the hands of each person as they entered the *temenos*. This act is known as a lustration, or lustral rite.

Most Pagan/Wiccan Traditions, at one time, instructed their initiates to take a ritual bath in preparation for ritual. I'm not sure that this is the common practice these days, and I would dare say that a good many Pagans take a shortcut with their ritual preparations. However, I would highly recommend, especially for Neo-Hellenic rites, that these old customs be reinstated in individual and group practice.

PARTICIPATION BY ALL

Each person in the ritual should be an active participant. One way that many Greek ritual groups accomplish this is by having each participant throw a handful of barley on the altar.

RITUAL CLOTHING

As mentioned above, the donning of clean, special clothing for ritual was a common practice, even among the Greeks. We're perfectly accustomed to the idea of "putting on our Sunday best" in the US. At some point, anyone with a remotely Christian background has undergone the ritual of shopping for a new Easter dress or suit, and similar customs permeate Jewish tradition. Even as Pagans, we largely embrace the concept of making and wearing special robes in our rituals.

For the purpose of a Hellenic ritual, one should also put on clean, special clothing and adornments. Though they do not have to be different in any way from your street clothes, you may find that you want to give those particular clothes/robes a Greek spin, as well. By so doing, you will be shifting your attention to the overall tone and demeanor of the rite to come.

The two basic garments that we'll discuss are the *khiton* and the *himation*. Both can be made of any natural fiber, but linen and cotton are the most common.

The *Khiton*:

1. Begin with a 72" by 60" length of fabric. It can be any color you like, as the Greeks had a particular fondness for color.
2. Fold this rectangle in half so that you have a double thickness of fabric that measures 72" by 30".
3. Position the open end on your dexterous side. You may sew this side shut if you

17

like, but it isn't entirely necessary. If you choose to leave it un-sewn, you can layer the back over the front slightly to keep the garment closed.

4. Pull the top of the back section of fabric slightly over the front and pin in place with two attractive pins. You may also sew the fabric in place. In either case, the fastenings should be located at approximately equal thirds across the top. You now have a neck-hole and two arm-holes.

5. You can use either one or two cords to tie the *khiton* at the waist and under (or across) the bust. Look at Greek sculpture and art for inspiration about tying these cords and draping your *khiton* in a flattering way.

6. You can wear this garment long or short, depending on your tastes and the need for warmth.

Though the *khiton* is generally described as a male garment, the woman's *peplos* is nearly identical except that an additional flap of fabric hangs down in the front. Women can either wear the *khiton* as it is, or they can fashion a *peplos* for themselves by adding a foot or so of fabric to the top of the garment and folding this over into a flap as shown here.

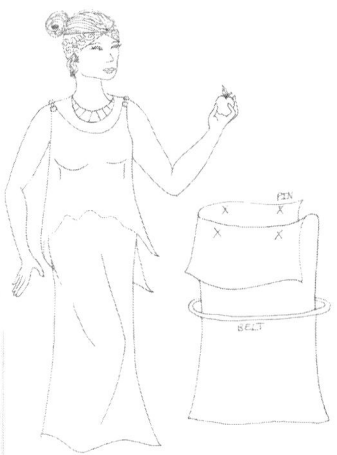

The Himation

1. Begin with a 60" by 120" length of fabric. Again, it can be any color, but you might like for this piece to coordinate or contrast with your khiton.

2. If you would like a himation that serves as a cloak, choose a heavier fabric. If you would like it to serve as more of a veil, choose something silky.

3. One popular way to wear this garment is to fold it in half lengthways, pull a little of the back portion over the top of the front, and pin it in place. Put your head and one arm through the hole and drape it as you like.

4. You may also wear the himation without the pin in a similar way by throwing one end of the fabric over the left

shoulder, looping it under the right arm, and placing the free end either over the left shoulder or carried on the left arm.

Women may also choose to play with the himation in a number of flirtatious and attractive ways. It can be draped around the shoulders, over the head, or around the body in

whatever way you can imagine.

Other Adornments

1. Adult men would always have worn a wreath of flowers or foliage, and women are also known to do so. Just avoid laurel, oak or olive, as these would have indicated

FESTIVALS AND RITES FOR THE GOLDEN ONE

favors and honors won by the wearer. Include these only if you have earned them in some way.
2. Garlands of flowers and leaves would also have been worn around the neck.
3. Sandals are certainly appropriate footwear, and it is safe to say that any would work. Greek sculpture and paintings seem to show such a variety of footwear that anything is fine.

The cords that act as the belts for both men's and women's garments can be of nearly any material and style. Play will color, texture, composition, etc.

CALL FOR SILENCE

Another common component in Greek ritual, and one you'll find included in the rites in this book, is the call for silence at the beginning of the ritual. An inauspicious utterance or off-topic chatter can be damaging for the many purposes of the rite, and the Ancients understood this.

HESTIA

Whether or not you are practicing Hellenic Pagan, you may want to consider the special role that Hestia is given in Greek culture. Hestia is the keeper of the hearth and temple flame, and she is honored in every home and in every ritual. You will notice her intentional inclusion in the rites included in this work.

Λατρεία της Αφροδίτης
CULT OF APHRODITE

Φεστιβάλ και αποχωρήσεις από τη Χρυσή
FESTIVALS AND RITES FOR THE GOLDEN ONE

Τη διακόσμηση του ναού και Παρεκκλήσι
DECKING THE TEMPLE, SHRINE AND ALTAR

Decorating the sacred space that you use can be a moving and meaningful experience all on its own. Choosing the objects that speak to an individual or group consciousness and have historical or mythological associations with a Deity, arranging them with an eye for visual and textual pleasure, and setting the mood are all acts of service to Aphrodite. Though Apollon is the patron God of the arts, Aphrodite is a long-standing source of inspiration for creative artists, and so it stands to reason that Her altars, shrines and other sacred spaces should be touched with Her beauty and ecstasy.

ALTARS

A friend recently said to me that every surface in one's home can be viewed as an altar, whether intentionally designated as such or not. When viewed through this lens, the entire home can be seen as a sacred place, and every surface takes on significance. Every section of wall and shelf, every counter and table relate to some God or Goddess, and when we focus our attention – and intention – on creating and maintaining a place of honor for that Deity, we are integrating both mysticism and spirituality into our daily lives. The Greek religion is like this in that religion and spirituality were so intricately and intimately interwoven in this way that there was no specific word that meant "religion."

CULT OF APHRODITE

Greek philosophy, though, did separate the sacred from the profane, and yet the sacred was always close at hand. The acropolis (or high holy city) was separate from the marketplace, but both were easily accessible to each other. The family altar, a specific and sanctified stone block, was housed in the courtyard or prominent room of a dwelling, but its purpose was only in receiving the family's offerings of food, meat, wine, incense, etc. In fact, the idea of idly draping a garment or placing a mundane household item on the altar would have been contrary to the space's sanctity.

If you desire the traditional Hellenic altar because you want to achieve the most authentic worship of the Greek Gods possible, you may want to establish an outdoor stone altar on which you do nothing but pour libations, or you may build an altar on which you can burn offerings safely. You could carve or paint words of dedication on the stone, such as "This altar is established for the honor and adoration of most beautiful Aphrodite."

A more convenient version of this concept, especially for apartment-dwellers, is to clear a shelf or tabletop of everything but a Deity image and a libation bowl. If, though, when all is said and done, you find that you prefer a more decorative and evocative altar space, I recommend the inclusion of the libation bowl, first and foremost, among your altar's accoutrement. The old Gods were almost universally called and honored with the spilling of blood, wine, honey, fruits, and other offerings. Be sure to give yourself the place to honor Them thusly. Also, be sure to make sure that your offerings eventually make their way outside in a respectful manner.

SHRINES

My definition of "shrine" describes it as a larger, more elaborate, and more permanent location than the altar may be. Where the altar may be reduced simply to its function as a place for sacrifice, the shrine is best thought of as a "guest room" for the Deity whom it honors. It is usually a decorative space that includes at least one image of the Goddess along with the libation bowl, but it probably also includes a number of symbolic representations and a few lasting offerings, such as jewelry, ribbons, art, etc.

There are a variety of reasons and ways to build and decorate a shrine and all are valid. Modern Hellenics don't have established public shrines to which we can make pilgrimages — or, rather, we have very few, and most of the ones we have access to were established as museums or artistic monuments. So, it makes sense to establish these places in our homes until we have the means to establish them more permanently and prestigiously in the world.

A wide variety of bases can be used in order to establish a shrine. Obviously, dresser tops and bookcase shelves can be cleared to make way for sacred items and images, but other surfaces can be used to surprisingly stunning effect, as well. A single curio shelf provides a great spot for a wall-mounted shrine. I'm quite a fan of such a shelf with three or four wooden coat pegs, giving me the opportunity to hang certain pieces of the altar display, such as necklaces or garlands. A tier of two or three shelves can provide a lovely layered look and give you space to separate items in a way that speaks to your sense of order (or your sense of artistry). Perhaps a statue of Aphrodite with several small attributes (like shells, a mirror and comb, and swans) could reside on the top shelf, while the bottom shelf holds a libation bowl and other offerings for the Goddess.

A baker's rack or an armoire can be used to create a stunning shrine to Aphrodite. These larger pieces of furniture can accommodate both large and small items, and they offer you a significant focal point for your devotions and offerings. I especially like the armoire since it can be closed and made private by the devotee, or it can be opened to reveal the beautiful treasures and mysteries within. This, to me, is so much like the nature of any Goddess that it makes poetic sense.

An outdoor shrine to Aphrodite might be established under an apple tree or rose bush in one's yard. Place a statue that can withstand the local weather along with a terra cotta or stone dish for offerings in a secure spot on the ground. Tie a few ribbons to the branches, not just as a pretty gesture but also as an encouragement to avian visitors who will claim the ribbons for their nests while incidentally helping to cross-pollinate your shrine's base.

Pay attention to the condition of your shrine. Don't let it get dusty or neglected. Clear out cobwebs and clutter as they accumulate. You may enjoy the look and feel of a few months' worth of offerings – dried flowers intermingled with fresh ones, faded pictures and poems, bits of ribbon and jewelry mixed together and forming the perfect picture of lovely decay. That's actually just fine, in my opinion, as long as we enter into that visual arrangement with intention. Of course, I'd still clear out the dead flowers every so often to make room for the new. Perhaps you'll choose specific festivals or devotional dates on which to clean the sacred spaces of your home.

TEMPLES

If you are fortunate enough to have a dedicated temple space that isn't used for any profane or mundane activities, you are probably the envy of the Pagan community. The sad truth is that we don't, as a culture, have many groves and temples to which we can go for worship and ritual. The few we have are far from each other and far from many of the people who would choose to visit them. Journeys to such places are especially momentous occasions for most of us, akin to pilgrimages.

Most of us make due with converting our living rooms and bedrooms, our garages and back porches, and even tents in hospitable campgrounds into temporary temple spaces. There's nothing inherently wrong with this. It's the modern condition. A good many of us hope to inspire enough devotion to the old Gods to see the erection of physical, permanent temples in our cities and neighborhoods, but until then we can certainly honor the Gods in the nomadic fashion of yesteryear.

Whether we're using an indoor space or an outdoor one, I like to recommend paying special attention to the ambience and atmosphere when preparing for an Aphrodite ritual. Since ritual speaks to us on a symbolic level, it's important to include visual symbol, auditory symbol, and even olfactory (smelling) and tactile (touching) symbols and triggers. Hang garlands of real or silk flowers and leaves, drape silk or sheer chiffon and organza veils from both high and low points, bestrew the place with candles and rose petals, light incense, and play music. Be creative and sensual, and you'll surely do justice to an Aphrodite temple, even if it only exists in the physical world for a single glorious evening.

SYMBOLS AND ATTRIBUTES

When choosing the items to include in your shrines, altars and temples, I recommend taking a very personal approach. Ask yourself what says "Aphrodite, love, birth, cleansing, sensuality, sexuality, etc" in a visual, auditory, tactile, or olfactory way. What colors are evocative of these ideas for you? What types of music? Which incenses, textures, etc? Pull in those things that already speak to your subconscious, and don't rely solely on what you read from somebody else's lists. Not even those included here.

In fact, the following lists are really provided as a starting place. These are the symbols and attributes that I have found to have historical and artistic associations with Aphrodite, as well as the items and concepts that have personal associations for me. Some of these may work beautifully for you. Others may not. The key is to find what connects you to Her.

FESTIVALS AND RITES FOR THE GOLDEN ONE

STONES

Star-stones	Like star sapphires or other conical or rounded gems on which a star appears; these represent Her as Heavenly or Starry Aphrodite
Rose Quartz	Associated with love, it is a natural fit
Tapering Black Stone	On the island of Paphos, a stone like this featured prominently in the annual ritual for Aphrodite
Lapis Lazuli	This stone is often associated with the Goddesses Ishtar, Inanna, Astarte and Isis (all of whom are connected to Aphrodite)

SCENTS·

Tree Blossoms and Flowers	All of the blossoms and flowers mentioned in the "Plants" list contribute oils and incenses that are evocative of Aphrodite
Myrrh Frankincense	Both of these resins were attributed to Her worship by Empedocles

COLORS

Blue	For water and healing
Green	Also for water; fertility
Gold	Her belt; the sunshine that crowns Her; the golden apple; often called "Golden" Aphrodite
Violet	Often called "violet-crowned" – an allusion to the purple dye trades that brought Her worship to Cypress and Cytherea
Pink	For love, sweetness and delicate sexuality
Red	For passion and lust
Black	For mourning and Her darker aspects

CULT OF APHRODITE

ANIMALS

Doves	Often noted as a "sacrifice" to Her (may have been released in sacrifice); a nickname for Her priestesses ("red doves")
Dolphins	Appear in art; reminder of Her oceanic origins
Snakes	Seen more in conjunctions with Her predecessors (like Astarte), but still valid
Swans, Geese	Birds that link both sky and water
Birds (general)	Sparrow and swallow – Reminders of Her rule as Heavenly Aphrodite; also reminiscent of Her father's character as the Sky God
Clams, Starfish	Sea creatures of all manner reclaim Her watery birth; this includes sea "monsters" (as several fanciful sea creatures have been shown to be subdued by Her)
Fish	She was said to metamorphose into a fish at one point
Turtles	Show up in art and sculpture
Hares	Probably due to fertility aspects

SHAPES/SYMBOLS

Pearls	Jewels of the sea, Aphrodite's birthplace
Five-Pointed Star	The planet Venus traces this shape in the sky over the course of four years
Mirror & Comb	Symbols of beauty and femininity
Golden Girdle	Woven by Hephaestus, this belt makes Her irresistible
Golden Net	Also woven by Her husband, this net trapped Her with Ares
Number Five	Frequently recurs in Her paintings, sculpture and myths

FESTIVALS AND RITES FOR THE GOLDEN ONE

BOTANICALS

Myrtle	Daphne's transformation and Adonis's birth
Roses	Often thought of as the flower of love and passion; myth tells us that the rose was white until Aphrodite, rushing to save her beloved Adonis, pricked Her finger on the rose's thorns and stained it crimson
Mandrake	Called the "plant of Aphrodite" because of its association with physical lust and passion
Violets	"Violet-crowned" refers more to the dye-trade than to the plant, but the association still sticks
Anemone	Especially connected to Her love of Adonis because she transformed his blood into this flower
Apple	Between the golden apple that instigated the Trojan War and the apples of the Hesperides, this tree and its fruit have long been associated with Aphrodite
Lime	Fruit trees, in general, speak to Aphrodite's fertility; and the sweet blossoms bespeak Her beauty
Ivy/Vines	Symbolic of Dionysos, the ivy and vine are frequently shown intertwined with other tree limbs that are sacred to Aphrodite
Laurel	Symbolic of peace and truce; high honors
Vervain	Protective of marriage
Pomegranate	Symbol of the Underworld; one of the elements that connects Aphrodite with Persephone
Cypress	Associated with the island bearing Her oldest cult center

31

Λατρεία της Αφροδίτης
CULT OF APHRODITE

FESTIVALS AND RITES FOR THE GOLDEN ONE

PRAYER

Prayer has traditionally been a part of all religious practice, though it takes divergent enough forms from one spiritual tradition to the next, making it sometimes difficult to distinguish prayerful acts from speeches of invocation or magickal incantations.

Poems and plays have provided plenty of samples of a very clear style of prayer in Classical Greece. Furthermore, they have reinforced for us the importance of prayer in the Greek mind. Prayer was made regularly, and it was an opportunity for communication, petition, and offering. Indeed, prayer in this style was a bargain-making between mortal and Deity with customary speeches, patent offerings, and a distinct format that is easily duplicated.

It was a reciprocal agreement by virtue of the fact that the mortal offered something to the Goddess in exchange for the petitioner's request. A votive offering, then, was involved in order to ensure the Goddess's interest in the deal.

Reciprocity is at the heart of the relationship between Gods and mortals, in both ancient and modern Greek practice.

Of course, a devotee might also pray in order to sing the praises of a Deity, without asking for anything in return.

Λατρεία της Αφροδίτης
CULT OF APHRODITE

A SAMPLE PRAYER

> Begin by calling on the Goddess using various epithets that appeal to you or your purpose.

Aphrodite Acidalia
Emerging cleansed and rejuvenated from Your bath,
Ourania and Pandemos
Of heaven and of earthly concerns,
Aphrodite Aphrilis and Antheia
Opening in spring like a maiden of flowers —
By whatever name you prefer, Golden Kypriot,
Hear me!
Come to me from the shores of Cypress.
Descend from the starry heavens.
Come to me from those places you like best
And hear my request.

> Mention places sacred to the Goddess from which she might appear.

> State past deeds performed from both sides of your relationship with Her.

I have served you as a priestess for many years
And I have done my best to honor you.
And you have blessed me.
You have put love in my life and joy in my heart.
You give me pleasure and grace because I serve you.
I need your help now, violet-crowned Kytherea.
My dance ability has come to a plateau,
And I need my grace and sensuality within my movements.
Help my body to move with your fluidity,
To capture the attention of all who see.
For this boon, I vow to perform a dance of seven veils in your name
At a rite in your honor.

> Make both a request and a vow to repay that request.

Φεστιβάλ και αποχωρήσεις από τη Χρυσή
FESTIVALS AND RITES FOR THE GOLDEN ONE

Ημερολόγιο
THE · CALENDAR ·

Λατρεία της Αφροδίτης
CULT OF APHRODITE

Φεστιβάλ και αποχωρήσεις από τη Χρυσή
FESTIVALS AND RITES FOR THE GOLDEN ONE

Φεστιβάλ Ημερολόγιο
THE FESTIVAL CALENDAR

The following devotional and festival calendar was developed for use with the Cult of Aphrodite Asteria Starry Queen of Heaven. I should note, though, that there is no codified method or schedule of honoring Aphrodite in historical Greece or elsewhere. Much of what is listed here has been pieced together from numerous sources recounting divergent local traditions, and it is offered as a tool for helping interested readers to connect with Aphrodite as frequently and regularly as possible.

Some of the rituals are written as solitary practices, while others are clearly written with a group focus. Adapt in the ways that you need in order to address your own circumstances.

CYCLIC DEVOTIONS

The three devotional rituals included here provide a practice for consistent and intense contact with the Goddess.

FESTIVAL DAYS

The festivals included here have been reconstructed and re-envisioned in order to reflect both the historical roots of Aphrodite worship and to meet the needs of the contemporary polytheist. Though much of Her mythology takes place in the spring and summer months, She is also a Goddess of mourning, madness, winter and autumn. These rituals cross the entire calendar and span the full scope of Her nature.

A Note About Calendars

I have opted to use the Gregorian calendar dates for this work for a variety of reasons. One of the main reasons is that I am aware that the readers of this book will be approaching this current work from a variety of paths, not just from a Hellenic Reconstructionist background. The Gregorian dates are common to us all in this modern era, and that is a strong case for their use all by itself.

A stronger case for my Reconstructionist friends, though, might be that these festivals are often pulled from city-states beyond the scope of Athens and its well-known calendar. Trying to piece the many calendar systems together is simply beyond the scope of this present work.

Wherever possible, I've provided notes about the traditional timing of the festival in its historical context. You'll find this information in the "Background" section for each rite.

FESTIVALS AND RITES FOR THE GOLDEN ONE

Daily	Lustration	Personal anointing, cleansing and attuning to the Goddess
Friday	Devotion	Meditation and reflection regarding the nature and presence of Aphrodite
4th of each month	Sacrifice	A ritual of offerings
Feb 14	Feast of Eros	Celebration of romantic and erotic love
April 1	Rites of Peace	Aphrodite subdues Ares
May's Dark Moon	Anagogia	Aphrodite is put to sea
9 Days After Anagogia	Katagogia	After Her return from the Sea; invocation
3 Days After June's New Moon	Arrephoria	Athena's festival; a Mystery ritual
Summer Solstice	**Aphrodisia**	Bathing ritual of Aphrodite and Peitho
August 18	Vinalia Rustica	Honoring Aphrodite's sanctuary
Fall Equinox	Adonia	The mourning of Adonis's death
October's Dark Moon	Epitymbria	Deep mourning, madness and release
November's Full Moon	Symposium of the Hetaerae	Courtesans revel with men

39

Λατρεία της Αφροδίτης
CULT OF APHRODITE

Το Φεστιβάλ
THE · FESTIVALS ·

CULT OF APHRODITE

> DAILY LUSTRATION

BACKGROUND

A simple daily lustral rite (a cleansing by water) gives Aphrodite's devotee the opportunity to reconnect with Her in an uncomplicated, but highly symbolic and poetic, way at the same time each day. This daily devotional rite, then, affords us a way to bond deeply with the Goddess while invoking Her qualities into our own bodies and lives.

MATERIALS

> *Khernips*
> An anointing oil or perfume

PREPARATION

Ideally, you should be freshly bathed. The ritual works equally well whether performed in the nude or fully dressed. Rinse your face and hands in the khernips.

THE RITE

Stand in front of your Aphrodite altar, gazing at an image of the Goddess while picturing Her standing before you in all Her radiant glory.

Anoint your heart and say, "Your love rules within my

heart."

Touch your face and skim your hands over your body: "Your beauty shines upon my form."

Kneel and touch the floor: "I walk in Your grace."

Stand, roll your hands and say, "And my hands do Your bidding."

Bring your palms together at heart height: "For You are within me …"

Hug yourself: "…and around me."

Lift arms up: "Hail, Aphrodite!"

CULT OF APHRODITE

WEEKLY MEDITATION

BACKGROUND

The sixth day of the week, counting Sunday as the first, has long been associated with Aphrodite. In Romance languages, the name of the day still bears the imprint of the day's planetary ruler, Venus. The Spanish and Italian languages name the sixth day Viernes and Venerdi, respectively. The English name "Friday" evolved from the Germanic "Freitag," meaning either Freya's Day or Frigga's Day, depending on the source. Both are generally considered to be Goddesses of Love and Beauty. The Greeks called this day Hemera Aphrodites.

With the obvious association of the Goddess of Love to this particular day of the week, it only makes sense to acknowledge this day as Aphrodite's day of honor within every seven-day cycle.

The following ritual is mainly a devotional meditation, and it was adapted from the ThiasosDionysos yahoo group.

MATERIALS

 Candle & holder
 Myrrh incense & holder (any favorable scent)
 Matches/lighter
 Honey
 Libation bowl

FESTIVALS AND RITES FOR THE GOLDEN ONE

PREPARATION

Before beginning, take a moment to calm and center yourself. You might find that lowering or extinguishing the lights works best with the candlelight. Sprinkle yourself and the space with *khernips* and sprinkle a few barley groats on the altar.

THE RITE

Light the candle and speak Her name. Include an epithet if you like. Visualize Her standing at some distance from you but still within the ring of candlelight.

Light the incense and say Her name again, potentially with a second epithet that emphasizes another of Her aspects. See the sweet smoke curling around Her lovely arms, neck and face. She is coming closer to you.

Pour the honey into the libation bowl and speak Her name for the third time. See Her standing very close to you now, dipping a slender finger into the honey and tasting it with a smile.

You may sit, stand, lie down or even dance as you envision the following:

A golden mist encircles you, covering every part of your body and your ritual space. You see yourself as loved and lovely. You are standing in the waves on a sandy shore. You feel the soft and gritty sand shifting under your feet as the waves roll in and away from the beach in the endless dance. The waves caress and rock your body very gently. The wind blows through your hair, and the sun kisses your face. Enjoy these sensations and feel yourself cleansed by the sand, waves, wind and sun of Aphrodite's bath.

When you are satisfied that the meditation has come to a close and you have finished, say, "Thank you, Aphrodite, for your healing and cleansing touch. Help me to bring the love of your touch to those around me."

Extinguish the candle and make sure the incense is secure.

Φεστιβάλ και αποχωρήσεις από τη Χρυσή
FESTIVALS AND RITES FOR THE GOLDEN ONE

Μηνιαία Θυσία
MONTHLY OFFERING

BACKGROUND

Historically, the Greeks devoted certain days within the month to the honor of specific Deities. The fourth day of each month (which would've been the fourth day following the New Moon according to the Athenian calendar) was dedicated to Aphrodite.

This particular ritual is sacrificial in nature and is also a deviation of a ritual developed by Thiasos Dionysos. It is your opportunity to give back to the Goddess on a regular basis – a small payment for all She gives us.

MATERIALS

>   Khernips
>   Incense & holder
>   Lighter/matches
>   Offering (poem, hymn, roses, coins, jewelry, etc.)

PREPARATION

Before beginning, take a moment to calm and center yourself. You can incorporate candlelight and music into this ritual, if you like. You should rinse your hands and face and sprinkle the space with *khernips*. Throw a few barley groats on the altar and light a lamp or candle for Hestia before beginning.

THE RITE

Intone three or four of Aphrodite's epithets. Choose any you feel drawn to this month.

Say aloud, "You bless us with beauty, Golden One, that our lives might not be drab and joyless. You shine the light of love into our homes and hearts, Adored One, and help us to reflect that light into the world. You give us physical pleasure, Lusty One, and our bodies are enlivened by Your sensuality. I thank you and strive to enjoy and appreciate Your bounty."

Give your offering to Aphrodite at this point. You can offer something physical or something intangible. Physical offerings might include jewelry, coins or cash, semi-precious stones, roses, wine or mead, a mirror, make-up, or perfume. Intangible gifts might include poetry, music, dancing, singing, love-making and even masturbation. You may want to include an offering of incense in addition to whatever other offering you give, as incense was a traditional offering to Her in many places.

The important part of an offering is that the gift is something meaningful and significant to you. If you have no attachment to the object, if it cost you nothing emotionally or monetarily, if it is something you can give with no real effort on your part, you haven't made a sacrifice.

To make a true offering or sacrifice to the violet-crowned Kypriot, put some thought into the gifts that you give Her. Give from your heart, as these are the gifts that She accepts most readily.

Φεστιβάλ και αποχωρήσεις από τη Χρυσή
FESTIVALS AND RITES FOR THE GOLDEN ONE

Φεστιβάλ και αποχωρήσεις από τη Χρυσή
FESTIVALS AND RITES FOR THE GOLDEN ONE

Γιορτή του Έρωτα
FEAST OF EROS

CULT OF APHRODITE

Λατρεία της Αφροδίτης

BACKGROUND

This holiday falls on February 14, the day when many people celebrate the now very secularized feast of St. Valentine's. Though most people are happily unaware of St. Valentine and his story, most understand the celebration of love and romance that is abundant on this day. In fact, the figure most closely associated with this holiday in the average person's mind isn't the saint for whom it is named, but Cupid, the Roman equivalent of Eros, Aphrodite's son and the embodiment of erotic love.

The Cult of Aphrodite Asteria has taken some distinct liberties where this festival is concerned. Namely, we're using an entirely modern festival date in order to tap into the egregore that already exists in relation to this holiday. The Athenian calendar places the Feast of Eros in the month of Mounikhion, which is roughly April/May, depending on the exact date. Sarh Kate Istra Winter, author of *KHARIS*, suggests the 4th of that lunar month as a likely date, as this was a monthly date in honor of him. (Eros and his lovely mother share the date in common.)

Instead of the larger public festivals that many of our other "feasts" resemble, we celebrate the Feast of Eros as a private dinner party. We invite either our closest friends or our special beloveds for an evening of sensual music, food, drink, chocolates, love letters and gifts.

As such, we exclude some of the public ritual elements from this feast, like the pompe.

FESTIVALS AND RITES FOR THE GOLDEN ONE

MATERIALS

Candle (any color) & holder
Bowl of water
Incense & holder
Lighter/matches
Salt
Barley
Hestia lamp/candle
Red candle & holder
Pink candle & holder
Love notes
Pens and stationary
Chocolates
Wine
Jewelry and flowers for Aphrodite
Coins and semi-precious stones for Eros
Aphrodite icon
Eros icon
Gifts for friends and lovers

PREPARATION

Whether you're entertaining friends or lovers will determine the specific direction of your decoration, but your focus should be on providing a sumptuous and sensuous experience. You can make either the dining room or the bedroom the site of your "feast" – depending on whether you intend to have a feast of food or a feast of flesh. Then again, you can have a dual focus and move from one to the other.

Choose foods that are known for their qualities as aphrodisiacs – strawberries, chocolate, champagne. You might prepare dishes or full courses from *The New Intercourses: An Aphrodisiac Cookbook* by Martha Hopkins and Randall Lockridge.

Apply a keen eye to the "stage setting" for this feast. Use glassware and dishes that are special, pretty or have some sensual delight. Light candles, scatter rose petals, drape satin and velvet over chairs and side tables, and play sexy music (however you define it).

Either let your guests know in advance that there will be an exchange of love letters, or you can have them write short ones on the spot. If you prepare them with this information, also provide them a guest list so they can write one for every guest, if they choose. If you have them write letters on the spot, you'll need to make sure you have pretty stationary and pens available. Either way, you may want to provide a pretty basket or box on the altar or dinner table as a collection point for each person's love notes.

You should also let them know that they should bring a gift of jewelry or flowers for Aphrodite and that they can do the same for other guests, if they like.

Arrange an altar with images of Aphrodite and Eros in the primary site of your feast.

FESTIVALS AND RITES FOR THE GOLDEN ONE

THE RITE

As your guests arrive, give them each a heartfelt hug and kiss and greet them with words like, "Welcome, Beloved, to the feast of love."

Prepare the khernips and then sprinkle the space after each person has rinsed his hands.

Each participants throws a handful of barely onto the altar.

Light the Hestia lamp/candle.

Read the Homeric "Hymn to Eros" or write one of your own.

Homeric "Hymn to Eros"

I Call great Eros, source of sweet delight,
holy and pure, and lovely to the sight;
Darting, and wing'd, impetuous fierce desire,
with Gods and mortals playing, wand'ring fire:
Cautious, and two-fold, keeper of the keys
of heav'n and earth, the air, and spreading seas;
Of all that Deo's fertile realms contains,
by which th' all-parent Goddess life sustains,
Or dismal Tartarus is doom'd to keep,
widely extended, or the sounding, deep;
For thee, all Nature's various realms obey,
who rul'st alone, with universal sway.
Come, blessed pow'r, regard these mystic fires,
and far avert, unlawful mad desires.

Light the red candle and say, "Hail, Eros!"

Light the pink candle and say, "Even as Her lovely and powerful son is honored, so is the Kyprian – Mother of Love, and Love Herself. Hail, Aphrodite!"

Eat and drink and enjoy each other's company.

Between courses or before dessert, exchange love notes with each other. Each person should also write a message of love and gratitude to place at the bases of the Aphrodite and Eros images.

After desserts and sweets, present your gifts of jewelry, flowers, coins and stones to Aphrodite and Eros. After the Gods have received Their gifts, you can give gifts to your lovers and friends. This is also an appropriate time to make a prayer of thanks or petition to Aphrodite or Eros.

Continue enjoying the pleasure of each other's company, conversation, embrace and love for as long as you like.

As each guest leaves, hug and kiss them again, saying, "Go with Love, and return to me soon."

Φεστιβάλ και αποχωρήσεις από τη Χρυσή
FESTIVALS AND RITES FOR THE GOLDEN ONE

Ριτε οφ Πεαχε
RITE OF PEACE

CULT OF APHRODITE

BACKGROUND

The month of April is named for Aphrodite. "Apryllis" or "Aphrilis," one of Her epithets, means "to open" – as in opening the blossoms of Spring. April is a time for us to open to the freshness of new life and love.

April follows hotly on the heels of March, the month named for Mars. In fact, it could be said that April (Aphrodite/Venus) overtakes March (Mars/Ares) on April 1st. Ares, in fact, is said to be subdued only by Kypris, so it is no wonder that Her month should follow His. (This commentary is based on remnants of the Julian calendar, of course, marking this rite as a syncretic rite from Religio Romano.)

April 1st is the date for the Rite of Peace – the time when love overtakes war.

MATERIALS

   Liknon basket
   Candle (any color) & holder
   Bowl of water
   Incense & holder
   Lighter/matches
   Salt
   Barley
   Hestia lamp/candle
   Red candle & holder
   Blue candle & holder
   Honey

FESTIVALS AND RITES FOR THE GOLDEN ONE

Libation bowl
Feast food, drinks, utensils

PREPARATION

Decorate the temenos with symbols of both Aphrodite and Ares.

THE RITE

The pompe for this rite should be led by a man, or even a group of men. The feeling expressed in the procession is a war-like march accompanied by loud, steady drums and angry music. Dancing that accentuates martial poses and postures would be appropriate here.

Within the pompe, there should be a fire-bearer, water-bearer, grain-bearer and basket-bearer. These four functionaries should circle the altar once and then place their items on the altar's surface.

Prepare the khernips and then sprinkle the space after each person has rinsed his hands in the water.

Each participant throws a handful of barely onto the altar.

Light the Hestia lamp/candle.

Read the Homeric or Orphic "Hymn to Ares" or write your own.

CULT OF APHRODITE

Homeric Hymn to Ares

"Ares, exceeding in strength, chariot-rider, golden-helmed, doughty in heart, shield-bearer, Saviour of cities, harnessed in bronze, strong of arm, unwearying, mighty with the spear, O defense of Olympus, father of warlike Victory, ally of Themis, stern governor of the rebellious, leader of righteous men, sceptred King of manliness, who whirl your fiery sphere among the planets in their sevenfold courses through the aether wherein your blazing steeds ever bear you above the third firmament of heaven; hear me, helper of men, giver of dauntless youth! Shed down a kindly ray from above upon my life, and strength of war, that I may be able to drive away bitter cowardice from my head and crush down the deceitful impulses of my soul. Restrain also the keen fury of my heart which provokes me to tread the ways of blood-curdling strife. Rather, O blessed one, give you me boldness to abide within the harmless laws of peace, avoiding strife and hatred and the violent fiends of death."

Orphic Hymn to Ares

"Magnanimous, unconquer'd, boistrous Ares, in darts rejoicing, and in bloody wars
Fierce and untam'd, whose mighty pow'r can make the strongest walls from their foundations shake:
Mortal destroying king, defil'd with gore, pleas'd with war's dreadful and tumultuous roar:
Thee, human blood, and swords, and spears delight, and the dire ruin of mad savage fight.

FESTIVALS AND RITES FOR THE GOLDEN ONE

Stay, furious contests, and avenging strife, whose works with woe, embitter human life;
To lovely Kypris, and to Dionysos yield, to Deo give the weapons of the field;
Encourage peace, to gentle works inclin'd, and give abundance, with benignant mind."

Light the red candle and say, "Io, Ares!"

The ritual participants will link little fingers and dance in a circle around the altar. Everyone chants:

> Io, Ares! Io, Mars!
> God of battles, God of wars!

Start at a normal pitch, then get very loud and clamorous for at least a few refrains. Then, bring the volume back down and bring the circle dance to stillness. Everyone should still face the altar in the center.

A woman comes forward and lights the blue candle. She addresses all the men in the circle as she reads or recites the poem "Amor Vincit Omnia" ("Love Conquers All") from *Crown of Violets: Words and Images Inspired by Aphrodite*. She can simply look at them, or she can use touch and close proximity to further stir the Aphrodite energy amongst the group.

Λατρεία της Αφροδίτης
CULT OF APHRODITE

"Amor Vincit Omnia"

You sweep me away,
A bird of prey claiming the tender prize.
Off my feet and into your arms
Then into my bower
And the golden net
Of passion,
Of love.

My warrior brings hard battle
And conquest
Into every land.
But by me you are subdued.
The hardened ram ridden
By the dove.

The same woman pours a libation of honey into the libation bowl. "Hail, Aphrodite!"

Commence the feast.

Φεστιβάλ και αποχωρήσεις από τη Χρυσή
FESTIVALS AND RITES FOR THE GOLDEN ONE

Αναγογια
ANAGOGIA

CULT OF APHRODITE

BACKGROUND

According to *Harper's Dictionary of Classical Antiquities* (1898), the Anagogia was celebrated on Mount Eryx in Sicily, the site of an important temple of Aphrodite that brought Greek, Roman, Phoenician and Egyptian ideals of the Goddess of Love together in one place.

Not much information is to be found on this festival, except that the Goddess departs and returns nine days later. "Anagogia" refers to departure or "embarkation," where "katagogia" means return or "descent."

Aphrodite's doves are mentioned by Aelian in his *Historical Miscellany* as leaving and returning with Her. This could dually refer to the actual birds who inhabitant the island in large number while also extending metaphorically to the priestesses who were often called by this name. Aelian tells us that the Goddess left Sicily to go to Lybia.

Similar festivals of departure and return are seen in other parts of the Greek world for different deities. Dionysos and Persephone are both honored in this way. Dionysos, in fact, is honored in Priene in conjunction with Aphrodite, where the sailors are said to honor the Goddess of the Sea. She is depicted as leaving for Her travels in a boat.

MATERIALS

    Liknon basket
    Candle (any color) & holder or torch
    Bowl of water

Λατρεία της Αφροδίτης
CULT OF APHRODITE

> Incense & holder
> Lighter/matches
> Salt
> Barley
> Hestia lamp/candle
> Paper or wooden boats
> Origami doves
> Paper or wooden image of Aphrodite
> Feast food
> Picnic gear

PREPARATION

Make or buy a small boat out of wood or paper. You will be releasing this boat into a body of water, so the materials should be eco-friendly. Whatever material you choose, use it to fashion an Aphrodite image small enough to fit into the boat.

You'll also want to make origami doves so that each person can carry a single dove in the procession. You may make them from white or red paper, as there are references to Aphrodite's "red doves" (Her priestesses) in Classical sources.

The Anagogia should be staged at a body of water, preferably moving water like a river, stream or the ocean. However, ponds and lakes are safer locations to add floating candles, if you wish.

CULT OF APHRODITE

THE RITE

The pompe for this rite should be led by one person bearing the Aphrodite image and another bearing Her boat. Within the pompe, there should be a fire-bearer, water-bearer, grain-bearer and basket-bearer. These four functionaries should part at the water's edge, with two of them on one side and two on the other to form a "gate."

Every person in the pompe should carry a paper dove.

Prepare the khernips and then sprinkle the space after each person has rinsed his hands in the water.

Each participant throws a handful of barely onto the altar.

Light the Hestia lamp/candle.

The person bearing the Aphrodite image steps to the water's edge between the two columns made by the procession functionaries. "Aphrodite of the Deep Sea! You bring sailors back to safe harbor. You grace them with the beauty of sun and surf and song. You are the benefactress of fair voyage, and we honor You!"

The person bearing the boat comes forward. "All the Gods have their time apart, and now is Yours, our Epipontia. May our days pass quickly in Your absence, for all is bleak when Love and Beauty have taken their leave."

Play drums, flutes or other instruments while the image is placed in the boat and then set into the waves.

FESTIVALS AND RITES FOR THE GOLDEN ONE

Each person sends their doves floating on the water as the music continues. If you are using floating candles, have each person light one now and set it on the water.

Commence the feast.

Φεστιβάλ και αποχωρήσεις από τη Χρυσή
FESTIVALS AND RITES FOR THE GOLDEN ONE

Καταγογια
KATAGOGIA

CULT OF APHRODITE

BACKGROUND

Where the Anagogia celebrates Aphrodite's departure, the Katagogia celebrates Her return. This festival is held nine days after the Anagogia, and we are offered as few details from history for this festival as for the former.

However, since the word "katagogia" refers specifically to "descent," the Cult of Aphrodite Asteria uses this as an opportunity to interact directly with the Goddess. She is among us physically at this rite through the body and voice of a priestess who is a capable mantis.

MATERIALS

  Liknon basket
  Candle (any color) & holder or torch
  Bowl of water
  Incense & holder
  Lighter/matches
  Salt
  Barley
  Hestia lamp/candle
  Rose petals in various colors
  Wine & cup
  Privacy screen
  Golden sash
  Multi-colored himation
  Wreath or garland of violets
  Feast food

FESTIVALS AND RITES FOR THE GOLDEN ONE

PREPARATION

The priestess who will invoke Aphrodite will already be stationed near the water behind a privacy screen of some sort. She is adorned with an embroidered golden sash, a himation of various colors and a wreath or garland of violets. She will invoke Aphrodite into herself while the other participants are preparing for the ritual and conducting the pompe.

Because of the nature of the role played by this priestess, she should be very familiar and experienced with invocation. She should also have an assistant or attendant within the group who can see to her physical needs as she releases the Goddess. Because of the complexity of this role and its function, the group's Hiereia should invoke Aphrodite.

Participants can prepare questions or offerings for the Goddess, as they wish. This is an opportunity to interact with Her directly.

This rite can take place at the same body of water as the Anagogia, for continuity's sake. However, if the group or Hiereia prefers more privacy than that location affords, feel free to conduct it in your temenos.

THE RITE

The pompe for this rite should be joyful, as it is a celebration of Aphrodite's return and an opportunity to be within Her presence.

Within the pompe, there should be a fire-bearer, water-bearer, grain-bearer and basket-bearer. These four functionaries should part at the privacy screen, with two of them on one side and two on the other to form a "gate." The remainder of the group will form a semi-circle around them

Prepare the khernips and then sprinkle the space after each person has rinsed his hands in the water.

Each participant throws a handful of barely onto the altar.

Light the Hestia lamp/candle.

A speaker steps forward and says, "For nine days, Aphrodite, have you been away from us. Today is the appointed hour of Your return, and we wait expectantly for Your descent to this mortal realm."

Participants scatter rose petals in the area where Aphrodite will enter. They can also be used as confetti when she makes Her entrance.

As she is ready, the Hiereia steps out from behind the screen as Aphrodite.

The speaker offers Her wine. "Sponde!"

This portion of the ritual is entirely unscripted and will take whatever form the Goddess desires. She may have words of love, encouragement or advice for those assembled – either individually or as a group. She may grant boons or answer queries. She may just admire the beauty of the temenos if there is nothing else to be said or done.

The speaker offers Her wine again. "Sponde!"

Aphrodite will return behind the screen and the Hiereia will release Her while the feast begins. The Hieria and her attendant will then join the rest of the feast.

Λατρεία της Αφροδίτης
CULT OF APHRODITE

Φεστιβάλ και αποχωρήσεις από τη Χρυσή
FESTIVALS AND RITES FOR THE GOLDEN ONE

Αρρηφορια
ARREPHORIA

CULT OF APHRODITE

BACKGROUND

The Arrephoria is one of Athena's primary celebrations, but Aphrodite has a notable role within the rites. The festival comes from Athens and is celebrated on Skirophorion 3, which is roughly the 3rd day after the new moon in June. We try to stick to this date as closely as possible.

Erechthonius was Athena's son, born to Her from Hephaestos. He was part serpent, and Athena both hid and protected him within Her aegis. Later, he became the first king of Athens, the city named for and protected by his mother, and his name changed to Erechtheus.

The Cult of Aphrodite Asteria recognizes a very close bond and relationship between Aphrodite and Athena. Both Goddesses are descended from the Paleolithic bird and serpent Goddesses of the Fertile Crescent. Both Goddesses are mated closely with both Hephaestos and Ares in myth. The Arrephoria, for us, is an example of the close ties and friendship that existed between the two.

Classical historians tell us that the Arrephoria was conducted by two young girls between the ages of seven and eleven. Dressed in white and wearing golden jewelry, they carried a covered basket from the Erechtheum (the temple of Erechtheus and the genus locus of Athens) atop the Acropolis through a tunnel corridor down to the Gardens of Aphrodite below. The young carriers then bore something else back to the Erechtheum.

FESTIVALS AND RITES FOR THE GOLDEN ONE

In the basket carried by the Arrephoroi were the *Arreta*, or "unspoken things." No text mentions precisely what these objects were, though scholars speculate that Athena's peplos may have been among them. Some also speculate that the girls carried dew, gathered perhaps from the sacred spring along the passageway. Both of these speculations make sense from a mytho-poetic perspective, since semen (dew) and wool (the peplos) are directly connected to Erechthonius' birth.

What, then, are the other objects carried in the basket? Well, the Cult of Aphrodite Asteria keeps its Arreta as secret and unspoken as did the Athenians. Because cult Mysteries for a particular Deity vary from one locale to the next, we encourage you to meditate, speculate and otherwise discover the objects carried in the basket for yourself. It is proper that there should be variations from one group to the next.

Furthermore, only two women in your local group should know what these objects are – the Hieria Aphroditus and the woman who will be your priestess of Athena. For it is Athena's priestess who places the first set of Arreta, and Aphrodite's priestess who sends Arreta in return. No others are permitted to see the objects, and mythology provides examples of Arrephoroi going mad and being slain for having looked upon these "unspoken things."

And why are they unspoken?

The Cult of Aphrodite Asteria is lucky to have its own priestess of Athena within its membership, Natalie Long (whose book regarding Athena worship is forthcoming). Natalie and I spend long hours discussing the myths and relationships between our beloved Goddesses, and she offers her own savvy interpretation of this ritual.

According to her, the fact that Athena had sexual relations with Hephaestos and bore a child had to be kept secret. Athenian culture is based on the notion that Athena was a virgin. However, Athena was willing to share this secret with Aphrodite, Hephaestos' wife and Athena's own friend. So, wise, grey-eyed Athena sends evidence of Her child to Aphrodite, and Aphrodite responds with acknowledgment and support.

MATERIALS

       2 candles (any color) & holders
       2 bowls of water
       2 sets of incense & holders
       2 lighters/matches
       2 dishes of salt
       Kista (covered basket)
       2 privacy screens
       Arreta (secret objects)
       Offerings for Athena and Aphrodite

PREPARATION

This is a Mystery rite that is conducted by just four officiants. Two women will act as the priestesses of Athena and Aphrodite. The local cult's Hiereia is the most obvious choice for Aphrodite's priestess. Choose an Athena priestess from among your members based on criteria that make sense to you, but you should bear in mind that this role shouldn't change hands from year to year.

The other two functionaries in this rite are the Arrephoroi, the bearers of unspoken things. Since you may not have very young girls in your local group, choose the Arrephoroi from among your members in a way that feels right. You might like to have the two youngest women fill these roles, or perhaps you will choose the two youngest members, regardless of gender. Then again, perhaps age will not be a consideration for your group at all. However you select the Arrephoroi, know that these positions can be filled by other personnel next year.

The Arrephoroi should dress in white and wear golden adornments. The priestesses should wear emblems symbolic of their respective Goddesses.

No other group members will participate in this ritual.

Each priestess will prepare the temenos at which she is stationed. Athena's priestess should be inside a building or temple space, while Aphrodite's priestess will be stationed outside in a nearby garden or yard. Each temenos should be outfitted with a privacy screen, behind which are the Arreta.

THE RITE

The Arrephoroi begin the ritual with the priestess of Athena.

Both priestesses prepare the khernips and cleanse the temenoi in the usual manner.

Athena's priestess speaks to the Arrephoroi. "I charge you tonight with a sacred and secret task. Aphrodite waits in the garden for my message, one which no eyes but Hers may see. Will you faithfully bear this message, knowing that madness and death await any who pry into the holy matters of the Gods?"

The Arrephoroi answer.

Athena's priestess retrieves the kista from behind the privacy screen. Before she brings out the basket, she ensures that all her Arreta are inside and well covered.

She says, "Take this, then, to the priestess who sits in the garden, and heed my dire warning not to look at the contents."

The Arrephoroi take the basket, carefully, to Aphrodite's priestess. One of them says, "A message from Athena, only for you."

Aphrodite's priestess asks, "Have you looked within?"

The Arrephoroi answer.

Aphrodite's priestess says, "It is well, for the few who have dared the glance were struck with madness and flung themselves headlong into their doom. Such is the wrath of grey-eyed Athena."

FESTIVALS AND RITES FOR THE GOLDEN ONE

The priestess of Aphrodite takes the kista behind her screen and transfers the sacred objects so that she is now sending something different back to Athena. "Bear this back to the one who sent you, but do not look inside. Where Athena punishes with madness, Golden Aphrodite removes love and all hope of love. Go, and faithfully discharge this last duty."

The Arrephoroi take the basket back to Athena's priestess, who looks at its contents behind the privacy screen.

She returns and announces, "Our task is done."

Both priestesses make offerings to their Goddesses and secure the Arreta.

Λατρεία της Αφροδίτης
CULT OF APHRODITE

Φεστιβάλ και αποχωρήσεις από τη Χρυσή
FESTIVALS AND RITES FOR THE GOLDEN ONE

Απηροδισια
APHRODISIA

CULT OF APHRODITE

BACKGROUND

Though Classical sources admit to there having been Aphrodisia rituals in several locales in Greece, only scant information exists about two – the Aphrodisia that were held on Cypress and in Athens. The Kyprian festival, though, is the more detailed, historically

This Aphrodisia is known as a bathing festival, wherein Aphrodite goes to Her bath at Paphos. This is a source of regeneration and cleansing for Her, as it is the site where She first came upon the land, according to many of Her birth myths.

Peitho (Persuasion), whom Sappho and Aeschylus list as Aphrodite's daughter, is also honored during this festival. The icons of both Goddesses are taken in procession from New Paphos to Old Paphos in order to be bathed and adorned.

Classical writers say that this ritual included "instructions in the Mysteries of Aphrodite" and that the participants are given a measure of salt and a phallus. No specific description of the "instructions in the Mysteries" are provided, though some scholars note that these were bawdy proceedings.

We celebrate the Aphrodisia at the Summer Solstice. The Athenian Aphrodisia was the first festival of the calendar year, taking place on the 4th day of the new month following the Summer Solstice.

FESTIVALS AND RITES FOR THE GOLDEN ONE

MATERIALS

Liknon basket
Candle (any color) & holder or torch
Bowl of water
Incense & holder
Lighter/matches
Salt
Barley
Hestia lamp/candle
Aphrodite statue
Peitho statue
Rose oil
Necklaces
Garlands and wreaths
Fresh cloth
Sea salt in small bags
Phallus cakes
Wine
Libation bowl
Feast food

PREPARATION

You should have two icons of whatever size you like. The Aphrodite icon used in this rite should be the one your local cult primarily uses in ritual. The Peitho icon can be the same size or smaller. Any female figure will suffice for Peitho.

Purchase pieces of fabric for each of the statues and cut

them to an appropriate length and width so that they can be used as himations. Also, make or buy necklaces, garlands and wreaths to adorn the statues.

Pour a measure of salt into small organza, felt or leather bags so that each participant may receive one.

Bake phallus cakes using the penis-shaped cupcake pans available at adult novelty stores. You can also shape bread dough into penis shapes and give these to each celebrant.

This rite will take place at a "washing place" of your choosing. This may be the same body of water that you used in the Anagogia-Katagogia, your backyard swimming pool or a bird bath that your group has designated "Aphrodite's Bath."

THE RITE

The pompe for this rite should be upbeat and filled with frivolity. You can sing a chant like this one:

> Aphrodite, Queen of Heaven,
> Aphrodite, Queen of Earth,
> Aphrodite, bring us pleasure.
> Aphrodite bring us mirth.

or

> Enter grace,
> enter beauty,
> enter the heart into ecstasy.

or

> Acidalia, dea orea.

Within the pompe, there should be a fire-bearer, water-bearer, grain-bearer and basket-bearer and two icon-bearers. These six functionaries should lead the participants on a walk that is longer than usual, to bring to mind the distance between the new city and the old. They will circle the space one time where the participants will stand and then place their items on the altar or on the ground near the washing place.

The Hiereia steps forward and says, "You are preparing to enter the Rites of the Aphrodisia. This is a mystery ritual, and as a participant in it, you will be initiated into these Mysteries of Aphrodite. Everything that you experience and witness here is sacred. Mystery is not understood by those who have not experienced it, and the price paid for breaking the vow of silence is a high one. The price will not be extracted by anyone here, but by Aphrodite herself. Never break a women's confidence. Her wrath can destroy as completely as her love can heal. Will you honor the silence of the Mystery?"

All participants answer for themselves.

Hiereia says, "Then quiet your mouth and prepare to enter the Aphrodisia."

Prepare the khernips and then sprinkle the space after each

person has rinsed his hands in the water.

Each participant throws a handful of barely onto the altar.

Light the Hestia lamp/candle.

A speaker steps forward and says, "Lovely Aphrodite! You and your handmaiden, Peitho, come once again to Your bath, where You find both succor and regeneration. Here, we strip away the hurts and dirt and clothe You in the beauty that befits You."

Each person comes forward to bathe the icons and anoint them with rose oil.

Place the himations and other adornments on both icons.

Instructions in the Mysteries

The following section is just one idea that can be presented as The Mysteries of Aphrodite. Each local cult in ancient Greece had their own Mysteries, and modern practice can and should follow suit. Use these Mysteries if you like, but feel encouraged to develop your own section of ritual to use here.

The Hiereia speaks: "Perhaps you have never heard the story of Aphrodite and the Golden Apple. "

"It happened when all the Gods of Olympos were gathered to celebrate the wedding of Peleus and Thetis. One had been neglected. This one was Strife, and She would have Her presence felt."

FESTIVALS AND RITES FOR THE GOLDEN ONE

"So She took a golden apple and inscribed it with the words 'For the Fairest.' Three Goddesses, all having a valid claim, vied for the trophy. To avoid heartache, Zeus appointed Paris of Troy to decide who would win it."

"Each Goddess offered a bribe. Hera, Queen of the Gods, offered lands and power. Athena, the Wise Warrior, offered victory in battle. Aphrodite, mother of Persuasion, offered Helen as bride. He chose Helen, wife of Menelaus and most beautiful of all mortal women, and the Trojan War began."

"So, the Golden Apple rolled in, and competition, confusion, and contention began."

"But Lady Aphrodite uses love and beauty to heal these hurts and smooth these problems. Loving words can untangle confusion. A loving touch can ease contention. A loving smile can erase competition."

"So Aphrodite claims the symbol of the apple, and makes it Hers. Truly, Love Conquers All Things."

Pour a measure of wine to the ground (or libation bowl). "Sponde!"

As the salt and phallus cakes are distributed to each celebrant, the Hiereia says, "Salt water swallowed Ouranos' genitals, and the sea foamed in delight to bring forth Golden Aphrodite. Take this salt and this phallus, reminders of Her birth, and have joy and regeneration of your own through Love."

Commence the feast.

Λατρεία της Αφροδίτης
CULT OF APHRODITE

FESTIVALS AND RITES FOR THE GOLDEN ONE

VINALIA RUSTICA

CULT OF APHRODITE

BACKGROUND

The Vinalia Rustica is a Roman celebration that honors Venus' oldest temple, which was established by her son Aeneas, the founder of Rome. The traditional date provided for this festival is August 18.

Kyrinas in Cypress was said to be the Greek who established Aphrodite's first temple in Hellas, though no corresponding date is mentioned.

The Cult of Aphrodite Asteria likes to bring this celebration a little closer to home. We celebrate the founding of our own temples, shrines and sanctuaries of Aphrodite. This includes group space and private space.

Establishing your own Aphrodite shrine or temple on the Vinalia Rustica is also a great way to celebrate the holiday.

MATERIALS

    Liknon basket
    Candle (any color) & holder
    Bowl of water
    Incense & holder
    Lighter/matches
    Salt
    Barley
    Hestia lamp/candle
    Flowers
    Aphrodite icon
    New temple/altar decorations

Offerings

PREPARATION

You need a space dedicated to Aphrodite for this festival. If you don't have one, now is a good time to select one.

THE RITE

This is a fairly unstructured celebration. Take the time to clean your Aphrodite altar or shrine. Add decorations and adornments to the space. Make offerings to the spirit of the place itself and to Aphrodite. Sit within the influence of the space and enjoy it.

Λατρεία της Αφροδίτης
CULT OF APHRODITE

Φεστιβάλ και αποχωρήσεις από τη Χρυσή
FESTIVALS AND RITES FOR THE GOLDEN ONE

Αδονια
ADONIA

Background

The Adonia is a festival that is said to be instituted by Aphrodite Herself. According to myth, when Her young lover Adonis was killed, She vowed to establish a festival of mourning in his honor so that the world would not forget his death or Her sorrow.

We are provided a fair amount of information about the Adonia from Classical sources. We know that it re-enacts the funerary arrangements for the Kyprian prince, often by having women prepare small wooden images for burial. As they would for any other funeral, the women wailed and tore at their hair and clothing in lamentation. Of this, Plutarch says, "Those who cared anything for such matters were distressed."

Philostratus tells us, "the Syrians at the time of the festival Adonia make up [baskets of flowers] in his honour, growing them under their very roofs." The Suda, a Byzantine reference akin to an encyclopedia, informs us that lettuce and fennel were grown in earthenware pots in the Gardens of Adonis. Furthermore, the story of Adonis' death relates both the anemone and the red rose to his rites. As Aphrodite rushed to save Her young lover, She pricked Her skin on the rose's thorns, staining the white flower red with Her blood. His blood, She transformed into flowering anemones.

We celebrate the Adonia at the Fall Equinox. Historical references to the traditional dates are fuzzy at best.

FESTIVALS AND RITES FOR THE GOLDEN ONE

MATERIALS

Liknon basket
Candle (any color) & holder
Bowl of water
Incense & holder
Lighter/matches
Salt
Adonis image
White shroud for Adonis
Anointing oils
Flowers
Small shovel
Water jug
Wine
Feast food

PREPARATION

You can use any beautiful male icon that you like for Adonis. The Cult of Aphrodite Asteria prefers to make a new image of him each year using salt dough and herbs, as opposed to buying a new male statue year after year. We like being able to shape the dough in a burial pose, and we are happy about how easily he returns to the earth through the work of the elements.

To make salt dough, mix two cups of flour with one cup of salt. Add half-cup of cold water and blend until the dough is smooth. Add a few more drops of water, as needed, to make the dough more pliable. Add fennel seeds, anemone petals or other herbs to the dough before shaping it into a figure of Adonis. This recipe will air dry over the course of a couple of days. Don't bake it, though, as this level of hardening makes it difficult for the body of Adonis to break down properly after burial.

The shroud should be sized appropriately for the Adonis you made.

You will want to have a few essential oils on hand in order to "prepare the body." You might include myrrh, cypress and rose.

This rite can be changed to include only women, as it would have been conducted in some places in Greece.

THE RITE

Prepare the khernips and asperge the altar after each person has washed her hands.

Each participant sprinkles barley on the altar.

Light Hestia's flame and call for silence.

A man says, "At the death of Her beloved, lovely Aphrodite vowed that mortals would honor him each year."

The Hiereia says, "Memorials of my sorrow, Adonis, shall endure; each passing year your death repeated in the hearts of men shall re-enact my grief and my lament."

The same man says, "Let the women come forth to prepare his body."

All the women of the group gather around the icon to bathe, anoint and shroud it. They should make signs and sounds of grief, as if they were Aphrodite lamenting Her lover.
When the body is ready, a woman says, "He is ready for his journey. Let the men bear him to his rest."

The men come forward to carry the icon outside to the burial place. This becomes a funeral pompe with gestures of grief and sounds of mourning. The women carry the flowers and small shovel outside.

A woman says, "Prepare a grave," and one of the men digs a hole just large enough for the icon.

Read aloud the following portion of Shelley's "A Fragment of the Elegy on the Death of Adnis" or write your own elegy:

"I mourn Adonis dead—loveliest Adonis—
Dead, dead Adonis—and the Loves lament.
Sleep no more, Venus, wrapped in purple woof—
Wake violet-stoled queen, and weave the crown
Of Death,—'tis Misery calls,—for he is dead.

"The lovely one lies wounded in the mountains,
His white thigh struck with the white tooth; he scarce
Yet breathes; and Venus hangs in agony there.

The dark blood wanders o'er his snowy limbs,

"His eyes beneath their lids are lustreless,
The rose has fled from his wan lips, and there
That kiss is dead, which Venus gathers yet.

"A deep, deep wound Adonis...
A deeper Venus bears upon her heart."
The men place the image of Adonis in the grave and cover it with earth.

Everyone places flowers over the gravesite.

Make a libation of water and wine onto the grave for Adonis as he journeys within the Underworld.

Commence the funeral feast.

Φεστιβάλ και αποχωρήσεις από τη Χρυσή
FESTIVALS AND RITES FOR THE GOLDEN ONE

Επιτψμβρια
EPITYMBRIA

CULT OF APHRODITE

BACKGROUND

John H. Wells, in an essay distributed on the Internet, provides valuable information regarding some of the lesser known rituals and festivals in honor of Dionysos. One such ritual is an often orgiastic rite that happens to include our lady Kytherea. Though no date and very few details are available regarding this ritual, a modern Cult of Aphrodite might choose this opportunity to explore some of the darker aspects of both deities.

Aphrodite has a decidedly dark side that is generally overlooked by researchers and ritualists alike. However, several of Her epithets lead us to believe that the Hellenes acknowledged the frightening aspects of Her nature. Names like Androphonos (man-slayer), Area (armed for battle) and Melaina (black one) are clear indicators that these portions of Her nature should not be ignored.

The Cult of Aphrodite Asteria has opted to call on Her at October's dark moon as Epitymbria, She of the Tombs. Following September's Adonia, a mourning, grief-stricken and heart-sick Aphrodite pairs with a wine-maddened Dionysos as They explore the pain of loss that can come from love.

MATERIALS

    Liknon basket
    Candle (any color) & holder
    Fan
    Bowl of water

FESTIVALS AND RITES FOR THE GOLDEN ONE

Incense & holder
Lighter/matches
Salt
Barley
Hestia lamp/candle
Purple candle & holder
Blue candle & holder
Honey
Wine & glasses
Libation bowl
Feast food, drinks, utensils
Decorations evocative of death, decay and loss

PREPARATION

It's best to come to this ritual prepared to mourn that which you've lost. Perhaps you've lost a lover or loved one to death, distance or disinterest. Perhaps you need to mourn the loss of some part of yourself. Whatever the case, this is not a warm-fuzzy, happy-go-lucky rite, and you should be aware that some difficult emotions may very well rise to the surface of your consciousness. Furthermore, you may find that your method of dealing with these traumas tonight may be drastically different from the methods you would normally adopt.

This ritual is about giving yourself over to grief and heartache. It's okay to get dead drunk and cry your heart out. Really. It's okay to sit and be silent in the midst of noise while you lick your wounds in an anti-social way. It isn't your job to make anyone else comfortable tonight. It's even okay to lose yourself in decadent, hedonistic pleasure for a few hours.

As long as you're using safe, sane and consensual practices, you'll be fine. In other words, you can allow yourself to do something you wouldn't normally do. Just take precautions so that you don't do more damage to yourself. Push your boundaries, but don't push yourself off a cliff.

The temenos should be decorated with images that speak to your darker sensibilities. Black fabric, fake cobwebs, skulls. Use some Halloween decorations, but leave out the "camp." You don't want the atmosphere for this rite to seem silly, after all.

On the altar, place icons of Dionysos and Aphrodite, the Graces and the maenads (the women who followed Dionysos and gave themselves over to His madness). Use black, gray and purple fabrics. Set out dead or dying flowers and bare grapevines. Be sure to have a libation bowl on the altar. Include the supplies for khernips: saltwater and burning incense.

You may want to include images or mementos of death, as it has touched your life – obituary clippings, funeral programs, photos of deceased loved ones. This is a ritual about dealing with our ongoing feelings of loss, however deeply or superficially stored. Use artifacts that are going to evoke these feelings for you. The gift a loved one gave you before that fatal car accident. A stack of letters you received from a friend who has now abandoned your friendship. A dried rose from the flower arrangement at your grandmother's funeral.

FESTIVALS AND RITES FOR THE GOLDEN ONE

Celebrants may want to wear coarse fabrics or dark colors for their khitons and peploi. Perhaps they will wear bare grapevine or wicker wreaths – or some other spare and barren foliage – as adornments.

As this is a ritual involving Dionysos, participants may want to drink a glass or two of wine or grape juice before the ritual begins.

THE RITE

The pompe for this ritual should be a somber procession to the temenos. Play a slow beat on your instruments, reminiscent of a dirge. A singer can lead the following chant/song:

> "From the vine, we take some comfort
> as we struggle with our loss.
> We may stagger in our madness.
> We may cry out in our hearts.
>
> "Dionysos, see our madness,
> Aphrodite, hear our cries,
> as we lay our grief and sadness
> in the tomb beneath your eyes."

As the chant continues, each participant undergoes the lustration at the temenos door.

Within the pompe, there should be a fire-bearer, water-bearer, grain-bearer and basket-bearer. These four functionaries should circle the altar once and then place their items on the altar's surface.

End the song and prepare the khernips. Sprinkle the altar after each person has washed her hands.

Each participant sprinkles barley on the altar.

Light Hestia's flame and call for silence.

A ritual leader steps forward to speak the invocation to Dionysos. This role can be filled by ether a man or woman, but we should note that most of the Bacchantes were women. This person will light the purple candle and pour a libation of wine for Dionysos while saying these or similar words:

"Dionysos! Zagreus! Bromios! You give us the joy and oblivion of your deep, red wine, and we drink deeply. Dionysos, drunken and besotted, be with us this night as we dive into your cup."

Another ritual leader steps forward to speak the invocation to Aphrodite. This role can be filled by a man or a woman. He will light the blue candle and pour a libation of honey for Aphrodite while saying these or similar words:

"Aphrodite! Epitymbria! Melaina! You give us pleasure and love to soothe the hurts that Life inflicts. Aphrodite, grieving and saddened, be with us this night as we huddle together against our own grief."

The participants can take up their instruments again and play slow, sad music while everyone drinks wine. Live music is the best, as it is adaptive to the atmosphere on hand, but you can also play recorded music, if you like.

Everyone takes a turn stepping forward to the altar to lament their losses. As each person finishes his lament, he pours a libation into the bowl for Dionysos and Aphrodite while the other ritual participants toast their comrades' sorrows.

Allow the ritual's energy to dictate this rite's natural course. Don't force orgiastic experience or deep melancholy. Both of these extremes are only possible when group members trust each other and are in the head-space to allow it.

End the rite by having the ritual leaders step to the altar again. Each pours a final libation and says, "Hail, Dionysos! Hail, Aphrodite!"

Move on to the feast and the process of sobering up (or finding a place within the temenos to sleep).

Λατρεία της Αφροδίτης
CULT OF APHRODITE

Φεστιβάλ και αποχωρήσεις από τη Χρυσή
FESTIVALS AND RITES FOR THE GOLDEN ONE

Συμπόσιο εταίρες
SYMPOSIUM OF THE HETAERAE

CULT OF APHRODITE

BACKGROUND

The Symposium of the Hetaerae is based on a reference to an Athenian celebration involving Aphrodite in which "women revel with men."

The symposia were drinking parties which were attended by men and a mixture of Aphrodite's women that included both costly courtesans (hetaerae) and common prostitutes (pornai). An entire category of Greek vase painting depicted scenes from these drinking parties and are among the earliest known pornography.

The women were hired for a variety of skills, all of which involved pleasure of some sort. The courtesans were educated in politics, philosophy, art, and science and could hold conversations with the men in a way that well-born ladies destined for marriage were not usually permitted. They were also trained as musicians and dancers and provided these entertainments to their hosts.

We hold our symposium on or at the full moon in November, at which time it serves as a release from the mourning experienced at the last two rites.

MATERIALS

>Khernips
>Wine, glasses
>Honey
>Libation bowl

Food to share
Gifts for the courtesans
Condoms (just in case)

PREPARATION

Since this is a group rite in which participants may express intimacy – sexual or otherwise – begin the group's preparations by administering a vow of silence once everyone is assembled. The man whose home is being used for the symposium would administer this vow as follows:

"We have come, in this home blessed by the Kyprian, to partake of an ancient custom – the drinking party. The gentlemen of the house welcome the courtesans, and as an act of respect, all who are assembled here must vow not to break the silence of the rite with any who are not among us. I ask you now, before we begin, will you keep this oath?"

Those who are uncomfortable or unwilling are allowed to leave without judgment or anger. All who stay are expected not to talk about what happens at the symposium with anyone who isn't in attendance.

Following the vow, one member of the company should conduct the cleansing by sprinkling the *khernips* throughout the space. Pass the water so that each person can wash his face.

Light the candles and incense as everyone centers themselves and focuses their energy.

Λατρεία της Αφροδίτης
CULT OF APHRODITE

THE RITE

The chief courtesan reads a poem in honor of Aphrodite. Use a favorite piece by Sappho or Homer, if you like. You may also use the following piece, titled "Scarlet Woman" from *Crown of Violets: Words and Images Inspired by Aphrodite*:

"Scarlet Woman" by Laurelei Black

I wear the red with pride
for I am no plain matron.

When I take you into my
sacred
bedchamber
you will know that I am
Aphrodite's daughter,
Ishtar's pupil,
a woman of the light.

Let me lay you down
among the crimson and golden cushions
below the grape-colored canopy of
my bower.

Lie among the rose petals as
I enter your heart
and hold you in the eternal embrace
of the beloved.

FESTIVALS AND RITES FOR THE GOLDEN ONE

You will never leave me.
Our shared touch will
remain on your skin.
You will share me
with your lovers,
and I will visit your dreams.

I am your Muse,
your Sappho,
your Helen,
your Elissa.

Love me
and find bliss.

The Host makes a libation of wine into the libation bowl. The group says, "Sponde!"

The Chief Hetaera makes a libation of honey into the libation bowl. The group says, "Sponde!"

The Host addresses the assembled group. "Welcome, my friends, to the symposium. Eat and drink. Talk of art, politics, science, philosophy and theatre. Dance and revel, for this is our purpose tonight."

The Chief Hetaera addresses the group. "We courtesans are here to enjoy your company and divert your attention from the rigors of daily life. Our services are available to you, for a small price. You may bargain for a kiss, a dance, a shoulder rub, a walk under the stars or a few minutes of focused conversation. Any of this can be yours for the price of a small gift, a token of your affection."

Encourage participants to stay for at least one hour of revelry. At that time, celebrants may leave if they are sober or have a designated driver.

BIBLIOGRAPHY

Aelian. Historical Miscellany. tr. Nigel G. Wilson. Loeb, 1997.

Aeschylus. Suppliant Women. tr, Gilbert Murray. NY: Oxford University Press, 1930.

Alexander, Timothy Jay. Beginner's Guide to Hellenismos. Lulu Press, 1997.

Black, Laurelei. Aphrodite's Priestess. Indiana: Asteria Books, 2008.

Black, Laurelei, ed. Crown of Violets: Words and Images Inspired by Aphrodite. Indiana: Asteria Books, 2010.

Burkert, Walter. Greek Religion. tr, John Raffman. Wiley-Blackwell, 1991.

Campbell, Drew. Old Stones, New Temples. Xlibris, 2000.

Harpers Dictionary of Classical Literature and Antiquities. American Book Company, 1898.

Hopkins, Martha and Randall Lockridge The New Inter courses: An Aphrodisiac Cookbook. Terrace Publishing, 2007.

Karl Kerenyi. Athena, Virgin and Mother in Greek Religion. Spring Publications, 1952.

Kerenyi, Karl. Gods of the Greeks. Thames and Hudson, 1980.

Online Medieval and Classical Library website. "Hesiod, the Homeric Hymns and Homerica." http://omacl.org/Hesiod/hymns.html

Ovid. Metamorphoses.

Parke, H.W. Festivals of the Athenians. Cornell University Press, 1977.

Pausanias. Guide to Greece. Translated by Peter Levi. Penguin Books, 1979.

Philostratus, Life of Apollonius of Tyana. tr. Christopher P. Jones. Loeb, 2005.

Plutarch. Lives, Vol. I. tr. Bernadotte Perrin. Loeb, 1914.

Sappho. Sappho: Poems and Fragments. Bloodaxe Books, 1992.

Smith, William. Dictionary of Greek and Roman Antiquities. Harper and Brothers, 1843.

Suda On-Line. http://www.stoa.org/sol/

Syballine Order website. http://www.sibyllineorder.org

The Divine Sappho website. "Hymn to Aphrodite." http://classicpersuasion.org/pw/sappho/sape01.htm.

Theoi Greek Mythology website. http://www.theoi.com

Wells, John H. "Lesser-Known Dionysian Festivals." http://www.wildvine.org/dionysos_festival

Winter, Sara Kate Istra. KHARIS: Hellenic Polytheism Explored. CreateSpace, 2008.

Λατρεία της Αφροδίτης
CULT OF APHRODITE

Hymns to Aphrodite

SAPPHIC HYMN TO APHRODITE
Translated by H.T. Wharton

Immortal Aphrodite of the broidered throne, daughter of Zeus, weaver of wiles, I pray thee break not my spirit with anguish and distress, O Queen. But come hither, if ever before thou didst hear my voice afar, and listen, and leaving thy father's golden house camest with chariot yoked, and fair fleet sparrows drew thee, flapping fast their wings around the dark earth, from heaven through mid sky. Quickly arrived they; and thou, blessed one, smiling with immortal countenance, didst ask What now is befallen me, and Why now I call, and What I in my mad heart most desire to see. 'What Beauty now wouldst thou draw to love thee? Who wrongs thee, Sappho? For even if she flies she shall soon follow, and if she rejects gifts shall yet give, and if she loves not shall soon love, however loth.' Come, I pray thee, now too, and release me from cruel cares; and all that my heart desires to accomplish, accomplish thou, and be thyself my ally.

CULT OF APHRODITE

HOMERIC HYMN TO APHRODITE
Translated by H. G. Evelyn-White

Muse, tell me the deeds of golden Aphrodite the Cyprian, who stirs up sweet passion in the gods and subdues the tribes of mortal men and birds that fly in air and all the many creatures that the dry land rears, and all the sea: all these love the deeds of rich-crowned Cytherea.

Yet there are three hearts that she cannot bend nor yet ensnare. First is the daughter of Zeus who holds the aegis, bright-eyed Athene; for she has no pleasure in the deeds of golden Aphrodite, but delights in wars and in the work of Ares, in strifes and battles and in preparing famous crafts. She first taught earthly craftsmen to make chariots of war and cars variously wrought with bronze, and she, too, teaches tender maidens in the house and puts knowledge of goodly arts in each one's mind. Nor does laughter-loving Aphrodite ever tame in love Artemis, the huntress with shafts of gold; for she loves archery and the slaying of wild beasts in the mountains, the lyre also and dancing and thrilling cries and shady woods and the cities of upright men. Nor yet does the pure maiden Hestia love Aphrodite's works. She was the first-born child of wily Cronos and youngest too, by will of Zeus who holds the aegis, -- a queenly maid whom both Poseidon and Apollo sought to wed. But she was wholly unwilling, nay, stubbornly refused; and touching the head of father Zeus who holds the aegis, she, that fair goddess, sware a great oath which has in truth been fulfilled, that she would be a maiden all her days. So Zeus the Father gave her an high honour instead of marriage, and she has her place in the midst of the house and has the richest portion. In all the temples of the gods she has a share of honour, and among all mortal men she is chief of the goddesses.

Of these three Aphrodite cannot bend or ensnare the hearts. But of all others there is nothing among the blessed gods or among mortal men that has escaped Aphrodite. Even the heart of Zeus, who delights in thunder, is led astray by her; though he is greatest of all and has the lot of highest majesty, she beguiles even his wise heart whensoever she pleases, and mates him with mortal women, unknown to Hera, his sister and his wife, the grandest far in beauty among the deathless goddesses -- most glorious is she whom wily Cronos with her mother Rhea did beget: and Zeus, whose wisdom is everlasting, made her his chaste and careful wife.

But upon Aphrodite herself Zeus cast sweet desire to be joined in love with a mortal man, to the end that, very soon, not even she should be innocent of a mortal's love; lest laughter-loving Aphrodite should one day softly smile and say mockingly among all the gods that she had joined the gods in love with mortal women who bare sons of death to the deathless gods, and had mated the goddesses with mortal men.

And so he put in her heart sweet desire for Anchises who was tending cattle at that time among the steep hills of many-fountained Ida, and in shape was like the immortal gods. Therefore, when laughter-loving Aphrodite saw him, she loved him, and terribly desire seized her in her heart. She went to Cyprus, to Paphos, where her precinct is and fragrant altar, and passed into her sweet-smelling temple. There she went in and put to the glittering doors, and there the Graces bathed her with heavenly oil such as blooms upon the bodies of the eternal gods -- oil divinely sweet, which she had by her, filled with fragrance. And laughter-loving Aphrodite put on all her rich clothes, and when she had decked herself with gold, she left sweet-smelling Cyprus and went in haste towards Troy, swiftly travelling high up among the clouds. So she came to many-fountained Ida, the mother of wild creatures and went straight to the homestead across the mountains. After her came grey wolves, fawning on her, and grim- eyed lions, and bears, and fleet leopards, ravenous for deer: and she was glad in heart to see them, and put desire in their breasts, so that they all mated, two together, about the shadowy coombes.

But she herself came to the neat-built shelters, and him she found left quite alone in the homestead -- the hero Anchises who was comely as the gods. All the others were following the herds over the grassy pastures, and he, left quite alone in the homestead, was roaming hither and thither and playing thrillingly upon the lyre. And Aphrodite, the daughter of Zeus stood before him, being like a pure maiden in height and mien, that he should not be frightened when he took heed of her with his eyes. Now when Anchises saw her, he marked her well and wondered at her mien and height and shining garments. For she was clad in a robe out-shining the brightness of fire, a splendid robe of gold, enriched with all manner of needlework, which shimmered like the moon over her tender breasts, a marvel to see.

FESTIVALS AND RITES FOR THE GOLDEN ONE

Also she wore twisted brooches and shining earrings in the form of flowers; and round her soft throat were lovely necklaces.

And Anchises was seized with love, and said to her: 'Hail, lady, whoever of the blessed ones you are that are come to this house, whether Artemis, or Leto, or golden Aphrodite, or high-born Themis, or bright-eyed Athene. Or, maybe, you are one of the Graces come hither, who bear the gods company and are called immortal, or else one of those who inhabit this lovely mountain and the springs of rivers and grassy meads. I will make you an altar upon a high peak in a far seen place, and will sacrifice rich offerings to you at all seasons. And do you feel kindly towards me and grant that I may become a man very eminent among the Trojans, and give me strong offspring for the time to come. As for my own self, let me live long and happily, seeing the light of the sun, and come to the threshold of old age, a man prosperous among the people.'

Thereupon Aphrodite the daughter of Zeus answered him: 'Anchises, most glorious of all men born on earth, know that I am no goddess: why do you liken me to the deathless ones? Nay, I am but a mortal, and a woman was the mother that bare me. Otreus of famous name is my father, if so be you have heard of him, and he reigns over all Phrygia rich in fortresses. But I know your speech well beside my own, for a Trojan nurse brought me up at home: she took me from my dear mother and reared me thenceforth when I was a little child. So comes it, then, that I well know you tongue also. And now the Slayer of Argus with

123

the golden wand has caught me up from the dance of huntress Artemis, her with the golden arrows. For there were many of us, nymphs and marriageable maidens, playing together; and an innumerable company encircled us: from these the Slayer of Argus with the golden wand rapt me away. He carried me over many fields of mortal men and over much land untilled and unpossessed, where savage wild-beasts roam through shady coombes, until I thought never again to touch the life-giving earth with my feet. And he said that I should be called the wedded wife of Anchises, and should bear you goodly children. But when he had told and advised me, he, the strong Slayer of Argos, went back to the families of the deathless gods, while I am now come to you: for unbending necessity is upon me. But I beseech you by Zeus and by your noble parents -- for no base folk could get such a son as you -- take me now, stainless and unproved in love, and show me to your father and careful mother and to your brothers sprung from the same stock. I shall be no ill-liking daughter for them, but a likely. Moreover, send a messenger quickly to the swift-horsed Phrygians, to tell my father and my sorrowing mother; and they will send you gold in plenty and woven stuffs, many splendid gifts; take these as bride-piece. So do, and then prepare the sweet marriage that is honourable in the eyes of men and deathless gods.'

When she had so spoken, the goddess put sweet desire in his heart. And Anchises was seized with love, so that he opened his mouth and said:

`If you are a mortal and a woman was the mother who bare you, and Otreus of famous name is your father as you say, and if you are come here by the will of Hermes the immortal Guide, and are to be called my wife always, then neither god nor mortal man shall here restrain me till I have lain with you in love right now; no, not even if far-shooting Apollo himself should launch grievous shafts from his silver bow. Willingly would I go down into the house of Hades, O lady, beautiful as the goddesses, once I had gone up to your bed.'

So speaking, he caught her by the hand. And laughter-loving Aphrodite, with face turned away and lovely eyes downcast, crept to the well-spread couch which was already laid with soft coverings for the hero; and upon it lay skins of bears and deep-roaring lions which he himself had slain in the high mountains. And when they had gone up upon the well-fitted bed, first Anchises took off her bright jewelry of pins and twisted brooches and earrings and necklaces, and loosed her girdle and stripped off her bright garments and laid them down upon a silver-studded seat. Then by the will of the gods and destiny he lay with her, a mortal man with an immortal goddess, not clearly knowing what he did.

But at the time when the herdsmen driver their oxen and hardy sheep back to the fold from the flowery pastures, even then Aphrodite poured soft sleep upon Anchises, but herself put on her rich raiment. And when the bright goddess had fully clothed herself, she stood by the couch, and her head reached to the well-hewn roof-tree; from her cheeks shone unearthly beauty such as belongs to rich-crowned Cytherea. Then she aroused him from sleep and opened her mouth and said:

'Up, son of Dardanus! -- why sleep you so heavily? -- and consider whether I look as I did when first you saw me with your eyes.'

So she spake. And he awoke in a moment and obeyed her. But when he saw the neck and lovely eyes of Aphrodite, he was afraid and turned his eyes aside another way, hiding his comely face with his cloak. Then he uttered winged words and entreated her:

'So soon as ever I saw you with my eyes, goddess, I knew that you were divine; but you did not tell me truly. Yet by Zeus who holds the aegis I beseech you, leave me not to lead a palsied life among men, but have pity on me; for he who lies with a deathless goddess is no hale man afterwards.'

Then Aphrodite the daughter of Zeus answered him: 'Anchises, most glorious of mortal men, take courage and be not too fearful in your heart. You need fear no harm from me nor from the other blessed ones, for you are dear to the gods: and you shall have a dear son who shall reign among the Trojans, and children's children after him, springing up continually. His name shall be Aeneas, because I felt awful grief in that I laid me in the bed of mortal man: yet are those of your race always the most like to gods of all mortal men in beauty and in stature.

'Verily wise Zeus carried off golden-haired Ganymedes because of his beauty, to be amongst the Deathless Ones and pour drink for the gods in the house of Zeus -- a won-

FESTIVALS AND RITES FOR THE GOLDEN ONE

der to see -- honoured by all the immortals as he draws the red nectar from the golden bowl. But grief that could not be soothed filled the heart of Tros; for he knew not whither the heaven-sent whirlwind had caught up his dear son, so that he mourned him always, unceasingly, until Zeus pitied him and gave him high-stepping horses such as carry the immortals as recompense for his son. These he gave him as a gift. And at the command of Zeus, the Guide, the slayer of Argus, told him all, and how his son would be deathless and unageing, even as the gods. So when Tros heard these tidings from Zeus, he no longer kept mourning but rejoiced in his heart and rode joyfully with his storm-footed horses.

`So also golden-throned Eos rapt away Tithonus who was of your race and like the deathless gods. And she went to ask the dark-clouded Son of Cronos that he should be deathless and live eternally; and Zeus bowed his head to her prayer and fulfilled her desire. Too simply was queenly Eos: she thought not in her heart to ask youth for him and to strip him of the slough of deadly age. So while he enjoyed the sweet flower of life he lived rapturously with golden-throned Eos, the early-born, by the streams of Ocean, at the ends of the earth; but when the first grey hairs began to ripple from his comely head and noble chin, queenly Eos kept away from his bed, though she cherished him in her house and nourished him with food and ambrosia and gave him rich clothing. But when loathsome old age pressed full upon him, and he could not move nor lift his limbs, this seemed to her in her heart the best counsel: she laid him in a room and put to the shining doors. There he babbles endlessly, and no more has strength at all, such as once he had in his supple limbs.

'I would not have you be deathless among the deathless gods and live continually after such sort. Yet if you could live on such as now you are in look and in form, and be called my husband, sorrow would not then enfold my careful heart.

But, as it is, harsh old age will soon enshroud you -- ruthless age which stands someday at the side of every man, deadly, wearying, dreaded even by the gods.

'And now because of you I shall have great shame among the deathless gods henceforth, continually. For until now they feared my jibes and the wiles by which, or soon or late, I mated all the immortals with mortal women, making them all subject to my will. But now my mouth shall no more have this power among the gods; for very great has been my madness, my miserable and dreadful madness, and I went astray out of my mind who have gotten a child beneath my girdle, mating with a mortal man. As for the child, as soon as he sees the light of the sun, the deep-breasted mountain Nymphs who inhabit this great and holy mountain shall bring him up. They rank neither with mortals nor with immortals: long indeed do they live, eating heavenly food and treading the lovely dance among the immortals, and with them the Sileni and the sharp-eyed Slayer of Argus mate in the depths of pleasant caves; but at their birth pines or high-topped oaks spring up with them upon the fruitful earth, beautiful, flourishing trees, towering high upon the lofty mountains (and men call them holy

FESTIVALS AND RITES FOR THE GOLDEN ONE

places of the immortals, and never mortal lops them with the axe); but when the fate of death is near at hand, first those lovely trees wither where they stand, and the bark shrivels away about them, and the twigs fall down, and at last the life of the Nymph and of the tree leave the light of the sun together. These Nymphs shall keep my son with them and rear him, and as soon as he is come to lovely boyhood, the goddesses will bring him here to you and show you your child. But, that I may tell you all that I have in mind, I will come here again towards the fifth year and bring you my son. So soon as ever you have seen him -- a scion to delight the eyes -- you will rejoice in beholding him; for he shall be most godlike: then bring him at once to windy Ilion. And if any mortal man ask you who got your dear son beneath her girdle, remember to tell him as I bid you: say he is the offspring of one of the flower-like Nymphs who inhabit this forest-clad hill. But if you tell all and foolishly boast that you lay with rich-crowned Aphrodite, Zeus will smite you in his anger with a smoking thunderbolt. Now I have told you all. Take heed: refrain and name me not, but have regard to the anger of the gods.'

When the goddess had so spoken, she soared up to windy heaven.

Hail, goddess, queen of well-builded Cyprus! With
you have I begun; now I will turn me to another hymn.

Λατρεία της Αφροδίτης
CULT OF APHRODITE

HOMERIC HYMN TO APHRODITE
Translated by H. G. Evelyn-White

I will sing of stately Aphrodite, gold-crowned and beautiful, whose dominion is the walled cities of all sea-set Cyprus. There the moist breath of the western wind wafted her over the waves of the loud-moaning sea in soft foam, and there the gold-filleted Hours welcomed her joyously. They clothed her with heavenly garments: on her head they put a fine, well-wrought crown of gold, and in her pierced ears they hung ornaments of orichalc and precious gold, and adorned her with golden necklaces over her soft neck and snow-white breasts, jewels which the gold-filleted Hours wear themselves whenever they go to their father's house to join the lovely dances of the gods. And when they had fully decked her, they brought her to the gods, who welcomed her when they saw her, giving her their hands. Each one of them prayed that he might lead her home to be his wedded wife, so greatly were they amazed at the beauty of violet-crowned Cytherea.

Hail, sweetly-winning, coy-eyed goddess! Grant that I may gain the victory in this contest, and order you my song. And now I will remember you and another song also.

HOMERIC HYMN TO APHRODITE
Translated by H. G. Evelyn-White

Of Cytherea, born in Cyprus, I will sing. She gives kindly gifts to men: smiles are ever on her lovely face, and lovely is the brightness that plays over it.

Hail, goddess, queen of well-built Salamis and sea-girt Cyprus; grant me a cheerful song. And now I will remember you and another song also.

CULT OF APHRODITE

ORPHIC HYMN TO APHRODITE
Translated by Thomas Taylor

Heav'nly, illustrious, laughter-loving queen, sea-born, night-loving, of an awful mien;
Crafty, from whom necessity first came, producing, nightly, all-connecting dame:
'Tis thine the world with harmony to join, for all things spring from thee, O pow'r divine.
The triple Fates are rul'd by thy decree, and all productions yield alike to thee:
Whate'er the heav'ns, encircling all contain, earth fruit-producing, and the stormy main,
Thy sway confesses, and obeys thy nod, awful attendant of the brumal God:
Goddess of marriage, charming to the sight, mother of Loves whom banquetings delight;
Source of persuasion, secret, fav'ring queen, illustrious born, apparent and unseen:
Spousal, lupercal, and to men inclin'd, prolific, most-desir'd, life-giving., kind:
Great sceptre-bearer of the Gods, 'tis thine, mortals in necessary bands to join;
And ev'ry tribe of savage monsters dire in magic chains to bind, thro' mad desire.
Come, Cyprus-born, and to my pray'r incline, whether exalted in the heav'ns you shine,
Or pleas'd in Syria's temple to preside, or o'er th' Egyptian plains thy car to guide,
Fashion'd of gold; and near its sacred flood, fertile and fam'd to fix thy blest abode;
Or if rejoicing in the azure shores, near where the sea with

foaming billows roars,
The circling choirs of mortals, thy delight, or beauteous nymphs, with eyes cerulean bright,
Pleas'd by the dusty banks renown'd of old, to drive thy rapid, two-yok'd car of gold;
Or if in Cyprus with thy mother fair, where married females praise thee ev'ry year,
And beauteous virgins in the chorus join, Adonis pure to sing and thee divine;
Come, all-attractive to my pray'r inclin'd, for thee, I call, with holy, reverent mind.

Λατρεία της Αφροδίτης
CULT OF APHRODITE

Ο Αγώνας
The Agon

An *agon* is a competition, a challenge, a contest. An *agon* was a part of a poetic or dramatic performance. It was a verbal sparring between characters in comedy. It was an athletic competition or race.

In 2010, Asteria Books is initiating its first literary *agon* for the Hellenic community. Beginning this year, we will sponsor an annual literary contest for the entire Hellenic community. Each annual competition will be formulated around a theme or central question that each writer will address.

Submission categories will include:

- Essay
- Memoir
- Short Story
- Poetry
- Flash Fiction
- Photography
- Fine Art

Prizes include:
- free entrance to the Midwest Hellenic Fest (a three-day Hellenismos-focused festival retreat)
- cash prizes
- Hard copies of The Agon compilation

Visit www.asteriabooks.com/agon for more details.

Λατρεία της Αφροδίτης
CULT OF APHRODITE

ALSO AVAILABLE FROM ASTERIA

Non-Fiction

Aphrodite's Priestess — Laurelei Black
The priesthood of Aphrodite is not dead or dormant. It is alive, vibrant, passionate, and growing again. People are stepping forward from places like the US, Belgium, Brazil and elsewhere - stepping forward from the shadows of ancient temple ruins - to construct new practices of worship, celebration and transcendence based on acts of love, beauty and pleasure.

Aphrodite's Priestess (the 2nd edition - revised and expanded - of Laurelei's elegant and ground-breaking work, In Her Service: Reflections from a Priestess of Aphrodite) is the first book to offer readers insight into this re-emerging temple culture.

Crown of Violets: Words and Images Inspired by Aphrodite — Temple of Aphrodite, edited by Laurelei Black
Poetry, prose, painting and sculpture are among the oldest forms of devotion to the Goddess of Beauty. This collection of original poetry, invocations, photos, drawings, painting and digital art are heartfelt offerings of many of Aphrodite's contemporary worshipers.

Fiction

Temple of Love — Laura Britton
She was the ancient world's most famous female poet, writing lyrical verse for the men and women she loved. In this historical fiction offering by Laura Britton, see the life of Sappho through the lens of Aphrodite's priesthood.

WWW.ASTERIABOOKS.COM

5505688R00078

Printed in Great Britain
by Amazon.co.uk, Ltd.,
Marston Gate.